Praise for *Sent*

Heather and Ashley have crafted a beautiful picture of how God invites ordinary people to help those who are lost find a Savior. *Sent* will motivate any believer to embrace the mindset that playing a role in people finding Christ is not simply an obligation of a believer, but an adventure, a privilege, and a blessing. It personifies God's promise that we are all worthy to serve and called to a live a life of purpose that has kingdom impact.

TRACIE MILES
Author, speaker, director of COMPEL Training at Proverbs 31 Ministries

This is a great book that reminds us that we are all sent to be ambassadors for Christ, whether introvert, extrovert, or somewhere in between. It takes evangelism and makes it accessible to every believer by showing that it is a lifestyle of expectation and conviction that God is already ahead of us, working in the lives of those around us. The book invites us into the lives and experiences of this couple who not only write about evangelism but actually do it! If you are looking for a book on being a witness that is easy to read and faith-building, read this one and then use it in your group Bible study!

ERWIN W. LUTZER
Pastor Emeritus, The Moody Church, Chicago

Sent is a much needed and timely reminder that evangelism is a "get to do," not a "have to do"! Ashley and Heather remind us that evangelism is actually good for us, not just good for the world around us. *Sent* helps us see evangelism as the natural extension of who we are, an outpouring of where we are in our own journey with God. Ashley and Heather do a masterful job of moving back and forth through real and vulnerable story and timeless scriptural principles, both of which pull us into the heartbeat of God's great mission! *Sent* is exactly what we need right now, helping us see our identity and purpose in the world through the lens of our witness!

R. YORK MOORE
Executive Director/Catalytic Partnerships & National Evangelist, InterVarsity USA; coauthor of *Seen. Known. Loved.: 5 Truths About God and Your Love Language*

So many of us believe the gospel for our personal lives, but feel hesitant, nervous, and downright scared to share our faith with others. Heather and Ashley Holleman are here to help us all discover how joyful it is to be sent by God. With practical help and easy-to-apply suggestions, you will find yourself inspired to live your life like you believe that Jesus truly is the best news that this world has ever known—news worth sharing.

NICOLE UNICE
Speaker and author of *Help! My Bible Is Alive!: 30 Days of Learning to Love and Understand God's Word*; teaching elder, Evangelical Presbyterian Church

Sent introduces Christ followers everywhere to their lifelong calling of being "God's mailmen." Whether you are an introvert or an extrovert, Ashley and Heather share compelling stories of how to deliver God's mail to the people on your day-to-day route. Sent is a must-read if you are going to understand and live out of your true and identity in Christ.

DOUG POLLOCK
Author of *God Space: Where Spiritual Conversations Happen Naturally*

Sent is the guide to evangelism I have been searching for all of my ministry life! Heather and Ashley offer the reader the compelling why, the biblical inspiration, and the practical hows for any believer to share their faith in a winsome and winning way. What sets the book apart, though, are the stories of their authentic experiences living out the principles they are sharing. If evangelism is more caught than taught, then get ready to be infected!

JIM JOHNSON
Senior Pastor, Preston Trail Community Church; author of *Tough Stuff Parenting: Helping Your Kids Navigate Faith and Culture*

Ashley and Heather Holleman have an amazing ministry. Actually, they have two amazing ministries because they're so different from each other. And so, *anyone* can benefit from hearing their stories and insights. This book can be a great help for people at all different levels of confidence in reaching out.

RANDY NEWMAN
Senior Fellow for The C.S. Lewis Institute; author of *Questioning Evangelism and Unlikely Converts*

I am so thankful for Heather and Ashley Holleman inviting all believers into the fullest life of knowing and following Christ, a life that is sent. God has a mission, and frankly many Christians simply aren't part of it and, as a result, are missing their true calling. Their writing is genuine, passionate, and clear. I am thankful for this heartfelt explanation and call to the "sent life" and cannot wait to share it with my local church. We need this book as we join God in pursuing a life that is sent.

DEAN INSERRA
Lead Pastor, City Church, Tallahassee; author of *The Unsaved Christian: Reaching Cultural Christianity with the Gospel*

SENT

Living a Life
That Invites
Others to Jesus

Heather Holleman *and*
Ashley Holleman

MOODY PUBLISHERS
CHICAGO

Published in association with Tawny Johnson of Illuminate Literary Agency, www.illuminate literary.com.

Edited by Pamela Joy Pugh
Interior design: Ragont Design
Cover design: Faceout Studio, Spencer Fuller
Author photo: Light Ridge Studios

Library of Congress Cataloging-in-Publication Data

Names: Holleman, Heather, author. | Holleman, Ashley, author.
Title: Sent : living a life that invites others to Jesus / Heather Holleman
    and Ashley Holleman.
Description: Chicago : Moody Publishers, 2020. | Includes bibliographical
    references. | Summary: "What if your ordinary interactions with family,
    neighbors, and coworkers are actually invitations to adventure with God?
    Sent: Living a Life that Invites Others to Jesus invites you to grow
    joyfully with Jesus as you live out your true identity as sent to share
    Jesus with others. Heather and Ashley Holleman have fully embraced their
    identities as sent through nearly two decades of full-time ministry.
    With joy, they proclaim the name of Jesus knowing that God is always at
    work around us, that He is seeking and saving the lost, and that He is
    excited for us to do this work with Him"-- Provided by publisher.
Identifiers: LCCN 2020010498 (print) | LCCN 2020010499 (ebook) | ISBN
    9780802419798 (paperback) | ISBN 9780802498724 (ebook)
Subjects: LCSH: Evangelistic work. | Vocation--Christianity. | Christian
    life. | Holleman, Heather. | Holleman, Ashley. | Evangelists--United
    States--Biography. | Clergy--United States--Biography.
Classification: LCC BV3793 .H625 2020 (print) | LCC BV3793 (ebook) | DDC
    248.4--dc23
LC record available at https://lccn.loc.gov/2020010498
LC ebook record available at https://lccn.loc.gov/2020010499

Originally delivered by fleets of horse-drawn wagons, the affordable paperbacks from D. L. Moody's publishing house resourced the church and served everyday people. Now, after more than 125 years of publishing and ministry, Moody Publishers' mission remains the same—even if our delivery systems have changed a bit. For more information on other books (and resources) created from a biblical perspective, go to: www.moodypublishers.com or write to:

Moody Publishers
820 N. LaSalle Boulevard
Chicago, IL 60610

3 5 7 9 10 8 6 4 2

Printed in the United States of America

For those in your life yet to know Jesus

Contents

Introduction   9

Part 1: Believing That God Has Sent You

1. Believing That God Is at Work Around You   19
2. Believing the Gospel   41
3. Believing God's Titles and Job Descriptions for Your Life   55
4. Believing in Supernatural Power   87

Part 2: Living Like a Sent Person

5. The World We're Sent Into   111
6. What Do You See?   121
7. Gathering and Caring   131
8. The Easiest Questions to Ask   145
9. The Easiest Story to Tell   159
10. Inviting a Response   173

Part 3: Best Practices for Everyday Evangelism

11. Great Expectations   183
12. Great Surrender   193

Acknowledgments   197
Notes   199
Resource List   203

Introduction

This book isn't primarily a book about evangelism (although once you read it, you'll have what my husband, Ashley, calls "the *want to*, the *expect to*, and the *how to*" of evangelism).

It's actually a book about finding joy and intimacy with Jesus.

It's about finding and fulfilling a life purpose.

It's about finding a new identity.

Ashley and I, Heather, began writing this book because of the invitation to explain why we desire so much to talk with other people about Jesus. Although I'd been writing books on overlooked and unusual verbs in Scripture and speaking on identity in Christ, I'd always sprinkled into my messages incredible stories of introducing others to Jesus. And I realized this undergirding everything I do—everything I am—was another verb, perhaps the most important one of all. It's the verb in Scripture that connected me deeply with Jesus and with a joyous sense of adventure in talking to others about Him. It's the verb in Scripture that tells us everything about who we are, why we're here, what we're supposed to be doing, and most of all, with whom.

It's the verb *sent*.

As a Christian, I live a sent life. And so might you.

Sent represents the primary message God has built—and continues to build every day—into our lives individually and as a couple. Ashley and I live in the daily reality of being on an adventure with Jesus as He sends us specifically to our neighbors, coworkers, and strangers in our natural pathways to introduce them to God. We experience the intimacy of our union with Christ in this sent life that has marvelously and supernaturally shaped our lives for over twenty years. It's the best life. It's the life we were made for. But we didn't always live this way. God had to teach us a brand-new way of thinking.

A New Way of Thinking

Sent represents a biblical philosophy of living that reshapes the way we think about why we're here on earth and what purpose God has for us as worshipers and followers of Jesus Christ. *Sent* begins from a starting point of our identity in Christ; evangelism flows from *who we are* rather than inviting us into something more to do. As a result, we live as sent people not out of guilt, shame, or a sense of duty. Sent people naturally enter into evangelism the same way they eat breakfast or walk down the street. It's simply a part of who they are.

In other words, evangelism is not simply something more you do.

An evangelist is who you *already are* as part of your God-given identity in Christ.

Sent cements the idea that you and I as well as people in our churches and ministries aren't sharing their faith solely from a lack of training; rather, people don't share their faith because they often fail to understand their identity as sent ones. They see evangelism as something to *do* instead of something flowing from a God-given, God-declared, and God-empowered identity.

Fresh Motivation

Second, *Sent* motivates us by calling us to a supernatural adventure with Jesus. It's fun. It's exciting! It's something to enjoy with Jesus every day. As Ashley says at the beginning of our courses on living a sent life, "Evangelism is a *get to*, not a *have to*." After reading *Sent*, our prayer is that you'll wake up with fresh expectancy, fresh vision, and fresh zeal. You'll enter your day with a new purpose that will transform ordinary days to ones of true adventure. Living as a sent person has filled our days with unexpected personal happiness, curiosity, awe, and intimacy with Jesus.

A Practical, Daily Practice

Finally, *Sent* prepares you with practical, easy steps to immediately begin engaging those around you. You'll begin by first learning the three core principles that begin shaping your life, the four new titles and job descriptions for a sent life, and then what it means to depend on the Holy Spirit. You'll start by identifying five people who don't yet know Jesus, and you'll learn the seven ways to begin praying for them. You'll also gain some practical tips to live a sent life. Whether you're trying a "What do you see?" reminder or hosting a simple "Soup and Stories" night for wearied and busy families, you'll find plenty of ideas on starting, continuing, and finishing spiritual conversations. Each chapter ends with questions for personal reflection or group discussion and faith steps that allow you to practice those skills for a lifetime of living a sent life.

Meet the Authors

First, you might want to know a few things about us and why both Ashley and I chose to write this book together. Together, we bring nearly opposite perspectives on living a sent life. I'm the extrovert. I'm the one who can engage a rock in a spiritual conversation. I talk about Jesus in every place God sends me in a natural, unselfconscious way. Many people over the years have claimed that I have a unique and special gift of evangelism. Many people would even claim I'm unusually extroverted and someone whom God has enabled to engage others in spiritual conversations no matter what the setting (workmen in our home, the dentist, the grocery bagger, work colleagues, neighbors out walking). It's a joyful ferocity that makes me feel like a racehorse at the gate as I leave the house each day. I've heard people argue that this combination of spiritual giftedness and extroverted charisma doesn't apply to them. They would never talk about Jesus like I do. They don't have the gift. They don't have the social skills.

That's why I'm so excited that my introverted husband who claims God has *not* given him the spiritual gift of evangelism nevertheless regularly invites others into spiritual conversations and sees people pray to receive Christ as a result. He lives out the invitation in 2 Timothy 4:5 to "do the work of an evangelist" regardless of any sense of special giftedness for the task. As my polar opposite, Ashley still finds himself used by God to lead others to Jesus (most recently our eighty-five-year-old neighbor). As a reader, you might think you're the introverted person who finds having conversation in general awkward and stilted. You might be like the man in our class who said, "I'm not a social person!" or the woman who said, "I'm so glad Ashley is writing with you. I'm like him, not you."

Formally speaking, I'm trained as a missionary through my

involvement with the missionary organization Cru (formerly Campus Crusade for Christ) since 1997. Before this, I simply read my Bible and studied any resource I could—for example, the *Billy Graham Christian Worker's Handbook*—so I could tell others about Jesus as a teenager and then as a college student at the University of Virginia. I've never been particularly sophisticated or argumentative as I share my faith—even as I engaged other PhD students at the University of Michigan. My sent life—even now in my community and college classroom—has always been simple, organic, and true to my personality. But the truth is this: Because of this adventure of living a sent life with Jesus, I'm the type of person who enters a new space and feels this question bubble up in my mind: "Lord, who needs to know You here?" I also continue to keep a list of five people in my life I'm regularly praying for and engaging in spiritual conversations—a practice I started over twenty-five years ago.

I (Ashley) currently serve as the National Director of Graduate Student Ministry with Cru. I first began sharing my faith when I joined Cru's graduate student ministry during my first year of grad school at the University of Michigan. Before that, I grew up in, and was shaped by, a gospel-centered and missionally minded church.

However, before grad school I never personally embraced evangelism and living missionally. I knew as a Christian that I *ought* to share my faith, but I never really intended to do so. I expected that if I married and had children, I would share my faith with our kids and hopefully lead them to faith in Christ. Otherwise, I didn't expect to see God use me to lead others to Him. I did not yet know about my identity as a sent one of God. I didn't have any training for sharing my faith with others. And I assumed that given my introverted personality and lack of evangelistic gifting, I would at best stand on the sidelines to watch and cheer the few that God had uniquely called to share their faith.

This all changed during my first year in grad school when I saw my best friend there place his faith in Christ. I didn't just get to watch it happen. God used me directly to introduce Jesus to my friend and invite him to know Him personally. Afterward, I learned about my identity as a *sent one*. I learned all that I could practically about sharing my faith. This gave me much greater confidence that God could use me even though I don't feel I have the gift of evangelism. I began to reimagine the rest of my life as one where I would actively be involved in the sharing of my faith instead of remaining on the sidelines.

Finally, God began to transform my understanding of the personality He has given me. As an introvert, I am not naturally motivated by the vast numbers of people I could meet and talk with about Jesus. Actually, that possibility overwhelms me way more than it motivates me. Instead, as an introvert, I prefer to have a deeper connection with fewer people. God helped me shift my focus from seeing evangelism as engaging an overwhelming number of people to seeing it as something He and I deeply connect through as I have meaningful conversations with one or two people at a time.

He is also helping me see that as an introvert, I am one with whom other introverts may more easily talk about God. As introverts, we may be less overwhelming than our extroverted brothers and sisters in Christ. Heather laughs when I remind her about this. She knows it's true. She has a big personality and can gather a crowd. I'm more likely in the corner talking to one person.

Finally, and perhaps most importantly, God is teaching me that my personality doesn't have to define me. While introversion is no less valuable than extroversion, it can hold me back at times from engaging others God has sent me to. It doesn't have to, though. By the power of God's Spirit, I can step out in faith beyond my comfort zone and obey God as He directs me to talk with others about Him. What a joy it has become to trust God this way!

———————※———————

Together, we pray you find this book easy to read, easy to implement, and easy to use to train others in your community, ministry, and churches. We pray you feel closer to Jesus as you read *Sent* and that God increases your desire and expectation to see Him use you in marvelous ways in the lives of others for the rest of your life. Thank you for joining us on what's become the greatest thrill, the most beautiful way we worship, and the exciting purpose most of us have longed for all our lives: living as sent people.

PART 1

BELIEVING THAT GOD HAS SENT YOU

CHAPTER 1

Believing That God Is at Work Around You

My Father is always at his work
to this very day, and I too am working.

—Jesus in John 5:17

During a campus study break we recently hosted in our home in Pennsylvania, someone asked Ashley and me a meaningful question that more and more people have wondered about over the years. The event brought students and faculty together on a crisp autumn evening to watch football (this time the Eagles), play board games (Settlers of Catan), and share the frustrations of academic life (mostly involving time management).

A group of us sat huddled in our living room, some on couches, some on the floor, and some leaning against the wall. As we sipped hot apple cider and munched on pumpkin doughnuts from our local fruit farm, a professor's wife asked, "How did you become this way? What made you so bold to talk about Jesus?" The group leaned in to listen. I looked out at the faces of graduate students who, like me over twenty years ago, search for a way to shape their lives and walk with Jesus.

I told them how, as a struggling twenty-two-year-old woman—longing for purpose, hungry for God, and worried that I had somehow missed the abundant life promised in Scripture—I began to wonder why God sent me to live in the bitter cold of Michigan where the academic people around me were hostile to Christianity and mocked me in my classes for believing the Bible and for loving Jesus. I suddenly felt too young, inexperienced, and foolish for attempting to earn a PhD in English as a Christian. I thought I might quit graduate school and return home to the safety of my family in Virginia, but instead, I discovered a simple word in Scripture that redirected everything about my life.

I had been reading the book of Jeremiah and felt so deeply connected to this Old Testament man who also felt too young and too uneducated to fulfill what God wanted Him to do. God said this: "Do not say, 'I am too young.' You must go to everyone I send you to and say whatever I command you. Do not be afraid of them, for I am with you and will rescue you" (Jer. 1:7–8).

I circled that word *send*. In the cold of that afternoon in Michigan as I was far from home, uncertain of God's plan for my life and scared to declare myself as a Christian and help others know Jesus, I wondered if God was sending me, too. Had He chosen me for this particular place, with these people, for this time in history? And to make matters more confusing, I couldn't escape the odd reality declared in Scripture that I was an ambassador for Christ (2 Cor. 5:20), used to "spread the aroma of the knowledge of him everywhere" (2 Cor. 2:14).

What could these phrases mean? Did they apply to me? I felt both excited and uncertain about verses like Acts 1:8, which told me the Holy Spirit empowers people to be *witnesses* or Matthew 4:19 that presents the notion that when you follow Jesus, He'll "send you out to *fish for people*." These concepts began to shift everything about my sense of purpose. More and more, I thought of this idea of God sending me to people who needed to know Him. Could God use me? I wanted Him to. I asked Him to.

And He *did*.

I shared with those students and faculty in my living room in Pennsylvania, now twenty years later, that when I asked God to use me and to help me understand this sent identity, so many marvelous things began happening—not just in the English department but also during ordinary activities like going to the dentist. I would leave my house in the morning and ask, "God, could You really use me in the lives of other people to introduce them to Jesus?"

That day, I sat reclined with pink molding gel dripping down my chin because I needed a mouth guard for my incessant nightly teeth grinding. I had just learned how to share my faith using a booklet called *The Four Spiritual Laws*[1] that I learned through my involvement with Cru, but I didn't think God *would actually use me*. I didn't think He was at work anywhere around me. I wanted Him to be, and I wanted Him to use me, but I wasn't sure He really did things like that. I was still praying things like, *Is this actually happening, this crazy stuff about being an ambassador or spreading the aroma of Christ? Am I really a witness You have sent to fish for people? Is this happening?*

Oh, it was happening.

The dental hygienist asked how I had heard about their practice since I was a new patient. I told her I had come in desperation for a mouth guard, but I didn't have the insurance to cover the $800 cost for that kind of appliance. I prayed that God would somehow provide the money. In church that past Sunday, I had shared the prayer request with the man beside me. That man happened to own his own dental practice. He smiled at me and said, "Come to my office. I will make you that mouth guard for free."

I wiped some of the dripping gel off my face and said, "Well, I prayed that God would provide a mouth guard, and the dentist at my church told me to come here."

That was it. That was all I said. But God was about to use me in the story of that dental hygienist.

She leaned back, and tears formed in her eyes. "You pray? You pray to God? And He answers you?"

"Yes," I stammered.

She waited to hear more. I sat there for a moment, unsure and unprepared. I didn't know what to say, so I fished around in my purse for that booklet that presented the gospel. I asked, "Has anyone ever told you how you can know God personally, too?"

"No," she cried. "But I want to know!"

God was working, and He chose to use a poor graduate student who was so stressed out that she ground her teeth to nubbins.

I reminded her that I was new to all this sharing my faith stuff, and I didn't really know what I was doing, but I would try my best to share with her the good news of knowing Jesus Christ. I fumbled through the presentation: I began by telling her God loved her and offered a wonderful plan for her life. I read to her John 10:10 and how Jesus offers abundant life. I also read John 3:16 explaining that God loved us so much He sent Jesus to die for us. I then told her that we're sinners who were designed to know God but how our sin keeps us from Him. Third, I shared the good news that Jesus came to pay the penalty for our sin by dying on the cross and offering forgiveness if we accept the free gift of salvation. Last, I said that every person needed to individually receive Jesus—by faith—and accept this free gift.

I felt so nervous. I'm pretty sure I was shaking. But I read the booklet and told her she could pray the suggested prayer at the end where you express your desire to begin your life with Christ. I wrote down my phone number so we could talk more. That evening, my phone rang, and it was the hygienist. Her happy voice exclaimed, "I prayed that prayer! Now what should I do?" I invited her to church with me, and she began her spiritual journey all because of teeth grinding. I think of the awkwardness of the whole thing, including the dripping pink plaster and my stumbling presentation. But it didn't matter. God was working, and He chose to use a poor graduate student who was so stressed out that she ground her teeth to nubbins.

That evening the students and professors laughed as I shared the story and smiled about how God used my teeth grinding for His purposes. But I continued sharing in our living room that it wasn't just that dental hygienist who made me realize God was sending me to people. It was because of the students who came to my office asking how I knew the purpose of my life. I'd hand out copies of Josh McDowell's *More Than a Carpenter* to spiritually seeking students. One returned and said he'd surrendered his life to Christ.

It was because of the graduate students who asked me to explain my strange joy or approached me to ask about their personal problems—like the one who said, "You have an aura about you. Who is your spirit-guide?" As I shared about the Holy Spirit indwelling me as my "spirit-guide," she said, "Can you help me? I don't understand what I do. I don't do the things I want to do, and I do the things I don't want to do. What's wrong with me?" I had just read Romans 7 where Paul discusses the same problem, and that began the starting point to talk about Jesus.

It was because of the Taiwanese students I met who learned about Jesus for the first time and gave their lives to Him when they understood they didn't have to work to earn God's favor. It was because of the night it snowed, and I missed an appointment with a woman I had been praying for. I said to the Lord, "How can You send me if I'm trapped in the snow? You'll have to bring people to me if I can't go to them." My doorbell rang, and the woman stood on my doorstep. She had bravely taken a taxi ride through a blizzard to meet me and talk about Jesus. Day after day in Michigan, I began to see that God was at work to draw people to Himself, He chooses to use people to lead others to Jesus, and that God continually invited me into the work of evangelism whether I was reclining in a dental chair, sitting in a classroom, or walking around in the natural pathways of my day.

"So that's how it all began," I concluded. And God was teaching my now-husband, Ashley, the same principles. In our living room that night, Ashley shared his own stories of God using him in the lives of others and the way God was teaching Him to live a sent life. In fact, these principles shaped our lives then and continue to direct everything we do now in our lives in Pennsylvania.

The graduate students and professors were silent for a moment. Then, some said, "That's amazing" or "I want to live like this."

A month later, I spoke to them at the weekly campus meeting for Christian graduate students on living a sent life. This time, they took notes to begin internalizing the core principles of a sent life.

THREE CORE PRINCIPLES OF A SENT LIFE

PRINCIPLE 1: *God is always at work to draw people to Himself.*

PRINCIPLE 2: *God uses people to lead others to Jesus.*

PRINCIPLE 3: *God continually invites us into the work of evangelism.*

Just as Ashley and I learned at Michigan, right now, in whatever setting you find yourself, God is still working to rescue people, He chooses to use people to accomplish this mission with Him, and He now invites you into your greatest life's work of telling others about Jesus.

Most important, Ashley and I have learned that talking about Jesus with others is a natural extension of who someone is in Christ as they cooperate with the Holy Spirit. Evangelism as *communion with God* changed everything about us: our marriage, our careers, and how we, to this very moment, conduct ourselves in our family, neighborhood, and workplace. The focus of our lives became this sent identity that provided the foundation for our three core principles.

PRINCIPLE 1:

God is always at work to draw people to Himself.

In just two phone calls, God reminded me of a vital truth about Himself as a God who is *always at work*. It happened because of a tearful call to a United Airlines customer service representative.

My hand trembled as I held the phone. After an already exhausting and stressful trip for a speaking event, my homesick heart couldn't handle one more thing going wrong. I fought back the tears and anger as I apologized to the voice on the phone. I stammered, "I'm usually not like this. I'm just so ready to get home. Why did the airline cancel my flight? Please help me. I've got to get home!" I prayed and begged God to intervene.

You won't always hear Me, but I am here working. Stay on the line. I am here. You might not hear anything, but I am working.

The agent pulled up the original reservation while I waited in silence. The voice on the line assured me that I would be rebooked and would arrive home on time.

And then the voice said something that settled my heart and powerfully reminded me about God's nature. The calm voice said this: "It's going to be quiet on the line. You won't hear me. You won't hear anything. But I am here. I am working. I am making this right. Stay on the line. Remember, you won't hear me, but I am here working." I imagined I was hearing the faintest whisper of her fingers on a keyboard. Several long minutes passed. I occasionally whispered, "Are you still there?"

The agent would patiently say, "I'm still here. I'm working."

I smiled as I thought about God.

You won't always hear Me, but I am here working.

Stay on the line. I am here. You might not hear anything, but I am working.

I (Heather) sometimes wake up in the morning, and it doesn't feel like God is working. I don't sense His presence, and I find no evidence that He's working in the lives of those I'm praying come to know Jesus. How do I step out into a world that feels dull and devoid of spiritual movement or revelation? I remember the day I called my friend and found myself complaining about life in our town. Life felt slow and uneventful that week, and I said to her, "Sometimes I just want to move somewhere else! Why am I still here?"

She said, "Well, because God is still at work here. The Father is always at work." Her words reminded me of the unseen reality that God was working whether I perceived it or not.

Sent people embrace the often-unseen reality but nevertheless operative principle that God is always at work. And what kind of work is this? Consider these five moments in Scripture that talk about God at work as the foundation for Principle 1: God is always at work to draw people to Himself.

- **God is working.** In John 5:17 Jesus explains: "My Father is always at his work to this very day, and I too am working."
- **God designed us to desire eternity.** In Ecclesiastes 3:11 we read, God "has also set eternity in the human heart . . ."
- **God draws people to Jesus.** Jesus says in John 6:44 that "No one can come to me unless the Father who sent me draws them . . ."
- **The Holy Spirit is always testifying about Jesus.** In John 15:26, Jesus tells us, "When the Advocate comes, whom I will send to you from the Father—the Spirit of truth who goes out from the Father—he will testify about me."

- **Jesus came to seek and save the lost. That's what Jesus is still doing.** Luke 19:10 tell us: "For the Son of Man came to seek and to save the lost."

Think about the people around you. What difference would it make to know that God was working there? What if you believed God was orchestrating events to position you with people who need Him? He might also be sending others, and you exist as an important person—for a specific time—to help someone on their spiritual journey. If God is working; if He has put concerns about eternity into the human heart; if He draws people to Jesus; if the Holy Spirit is testifying about Jesus; and if the nature of Jesus is to seek and save the lost, then we approach conversations with other people with boldness and expectation.

At this very moment, Jesus is seeking and saving the lost. He is the Good Shepherd who continually searches after the lost sheep— those who don't yet know Him (Luke 15:3–7). And the Father is drawing people to know Him. God, in fact, "wants all people to be saved and to come to a knowledge of the truth" (1 Tim. 2:4). As we understand God's primary work in the world today—to draw people to Himself—we begin to believe in a grander purpose for our lives on earth.

It's incredible if you think about it. God is building a kingdom for Himself. He is *rescuing* people, and He invites us into this adventure of seeking and saving the lost.

PRINCIPLE 2
God uses people to lead others to Jesus.

Once we realize God is always at work to draw people to Himself, the next core principle transforms how we see ourselves in relation to God's work on earth to build His kingdom. *He uses us.* When you understand that God doesn't need people (He can impart truth to our souls without people), it makes you wonder why God chooses to use people in the work of evangelism.

I (Ashley) recently understood more deeply how God uses us in the work of evangelism and why. As I studied Acts 1:6–8, I noticed something as the disciples talk to Jesus. We read:

> Then they gathered around him and asked him, "Lord, are you at this time going to restore the kingdom to Israel?"
>
> He said to them: "It is not for you to know the times or dates the Father has set by his own authority. But you will receive power when the Holy Spirit comes on you; and you will be my witnesses in Jerusalem, and in all Judea and Samaria, and to the ends of the earth."

Did you see what happened here? The disciples spent three years with Jesus as recorded in the gospels. They were the first to hear of His resurrection and see Him alive again. They spent time with Him for many days and no doubt had the best understanding of anyone of what was coming next.

But they missed it.

They thought the physical establishment of the kingdom of God on earth was the next big thing to happen, and so they ask about it. That's what's on their minds. But if you notice, Jesus doesn't scold them, but He does redirect their focus. He tells them to let God worry about the coming physical kingdom, but then He tells them that He has something else for them right then in the present moment. They are going to join Him in the greatest rescue mission the world has ever seen. God is going to save many people,

Before He called them to do something, He called them to be something.

and He is going to use them to do it. He says this to the disciples who were there, and He says it now to us: "You will be my witnesses."

But also notice that He doesn't just give them new actions to do or new tasks to go after. He gives them a *new identity*. He says *you will be my witnesses*. In other words, you will be my missionaries. Before He called them to *do* something, He called them to *be* something.

----------------------✳----------------------

Consider these five moments in Scripture that shape this second core principle of God using people to lead others to Jesus. Note the words in italics:

- **God gives us the Holy Spirit to become witnesses.**
  Acts 1:8: "But you will receive power when the Holy Spirit comes on you; and *you will be my witnesses* in Jerusalem, and in all Judea and Samaria, and to the ends of the earth."
- **God uses us to spread knowledge about Jesus.**
  2 Corinthians 2:14: But thanks be to God, who always leads us as captives in Christ's triumphal procession and *uses us* to spread the aroma of the knowledge of him everywhere.
- **God has given us a ministry to lead others to Jesus.**
  2 Corinthians 5:17–20: Therefore, if anyone is in Christ, the new creation has come: The old has gone, the new is here! All this is from God, who reconciled

us to himself through Christ and *gave us the ministry* of reconciliation: that God was reconciling the world to himself in Christ, not counting people's sins against them. And he has *committed to us the message* of reconciliation. We are therefore *Christ's ambassadors*, as though God were making his appeal through us.

- **Jesus chooses and appoints us to bear fruit for the kingdom.** John 15:16: "You did not choose me, but I *chose you and appointed you* so that you might go and bear fruit—fruit that will last—and so that whatever you ask in my name the Father will give you."
- **God created us in Christ to do the good work He's prepared for us.** Ephesians 2:10: For we are God's handiwork, *created in Christ Jesus to do good works*, which God prepared in advance for us to do.

As we begin to shape our identity as sent people, these five passages tell us something powerful about who God made us to be: we're witnesses empowered by the Holy Spirit; we're used by God to spread knowledge about Jesus; we've been given a ministry to reconcile others to Christ; and we're chosen and appointed for this good work of leading others to know Jesus.

PRINCIPLE 3
God continually invites us into the work of evangelism.

A mentor once told me (Heather) that God will never give a command in Scripture that He also doesn't give us the desire and power to obey. Once I realized that God was at work all around me, every day, and that He chose to use ordinary people to accomplish His mission to rescue people and build a kingdom for Himself, I understood better how to respond with joy to His command that now felt like an invitation to a great party.

You probably know this command well if you've been in church. It's called the Great Commission, quoted here from Matthew 28:18–20. I love the word "commission" because it means our "official charge"; it's a formal, important, and auspicious kind of word. We read this:

> Then Jesus came to them and said, "All authority in heaven and on earth has been given to me. Therefore go and make disciples of all nations, baptizing them in the name of the Father and of the Son and of the Holy Spirit, and teaching them to obey everything I have commanded you. And surely I am with you always, to the very end of the age."

I love this Great Commission because of two often overlooked concepts: Jesus commissions us with His authority, and He invites us into a calling that's rich with meaning and purpose *with* Him. He is with us—in all His authority—as we enter into this work of telling others about Jesus. You may agree with the first two core principles that God is at work and that He does, in fact, use humans to lead other humans to know God, but you may take issue with His personal commandment and invitation to *you* to do this kind of work. Does the Great Commission apply to you or just to the disciples? As we read the New Testament letters that come after the ascension of Christ, we know that nobody misunderstood this point. The followers who would come after those first disciples, as explained in Paul's instructions to the early church, would work as ambassadors and witnesses as part of their new identity as Christians.

When I understood this calling, it helped answer a nagging

question I'd had since becoming a Christian. *What was my purpose here on earth? What's my actual calling? What is God's will for my life?*

As I embraced the Great Commission as my purpose, calling, and God's will for me, my career became my avocation (my minor occupation) and evangelism became my vocation (my calling to a career)—and this was before I joined a missions organization to work full-time in ministry. Not many of us will become full-time ministers or missionaries. But each of us has a new vocation, right now, as those sent to proclaim the gospel.

The words of Jesus had been bringing me here all along; I was Peter who would leave everything to follow Jesus when He invited him to follow Him and go fishing for people. I was one of the seventy-two in Luke 10:2–3a where Jesus says, "The harvest is plentiful, but the workers are few. Ask the Lord of the harvest, therefore, to send out workers into his harvest field. Go! I am sending you out . . ."

This third core principle stems from five scriptural truths:

- **Jesus commands us to tell others about Him.** Matthew 28:18–20: Then Jesus came to them and said, "All authority in heaven and on earth has been given to me. Therefore go and make disciples of all nations, baptizing them in the name of the Father and of the Son and of the Holy Spirit, and teaching them to obey everything I have commanded you. And surely I am with you always, to the very end of the age."
- **Jesus invites us into the work of drawing others to Him.** Matthew 4:19: "Come, follow me," Jesus said, "and I will send you out to fish for people."

- **Jesus sends us on the same mission He has to seek and save the lost.** John 20:21: Again Jesus said, "Peace be with you! As the Father has sent me, I am sending you."
- **God sends us to preach to others about Jesus.** Romans 10:13–15: For, "Everyone who calls on the name of the Lord will be saved."

  How, then, can they call on the one they have not believed in? And how can they believe in the one of whom they have not heard? And how can they hear without someone preaching to them? And how can anyone preach unless they are sent? As it is written: "How beautiful are the feet of those who bring good news!"
- **God invites us to live as His witness.** Isaiah 43:10–12:

  "You are my witnesses," declares the LORD,
     "and my servant whom I have chosen,
  so that you may know and believe me
     and understand that I am he.
  Before me no god was formed,
     nor will there be one after me.
  I, even I, am the LORD,
     and apart from me there is no savior.
  I have revealed and saved and proclaimed—
     I, and not some foreign god among you.
  You are my witnesses," declares the LORD,
       "that I am God."

With these verses solidifying our invitation to the sent life—as we now know God is working and He uses people to lead others to

Jesus—we're about to understand a radically different way to live. As you shape your new life from the three core principles, you'll begin to see God work in powerful ways.

However, you might be among the 47 percent of Christians who, in 2019, reported that it was *wrong to share your faith with others*. This report from Barna may astonish you. The research shows that this particular group surveyed—the millennial population—were more likely than even non-Christians to *strongly agree* that "it is wrong to share one's personal beliefs with someone of a different faith in hopes that they will one day share that same faith."[2] When we realize the core principles from Scripture that God is at work, He uses people to lead others to Jesus, and He continually invites you to do so, it not only makes it *right* to share Christ with others, but it makes it an inevitable and joyful part of the Christian life.

Sent is now *who we are.*

Right now, you may feel hesitation and even fear about this new identity. And you might have the legitimate concern that you don't possess the gifting or personality we see in many other fruitful evangelists. I (Ashley) can certainly relate. As we noted earlier, Heather is extroverted and has the gift of evangelism. I am introverted and do not have the gift of evangelism. I have only grown in admiring how the Lord crafted and gifted Heather. I thank God for her continuously. However, I have also increasingly embraced that evangelism is not just for Heather and others like her. The opportunity to introduce others to Jesus belongs to me too, and to every one of us.

So I often approach God with this question: "God, can you really use someone like me?" *I know You use people, but can You use me?* I feel afraid at times. I feel insufficient a lot. I get it wrong more than I would like. Perhaps you have felt that way too. Or perhaps you have thought, "I've always wanted to start sharing my faith, but I don't think I'm that kind of person." If you have felt that way—or even if you haven't—I want to share a story that has most helped ground me in my identity as a missionary or *sent one*.

During one inglorious moment in my life, our younger daughter asked to help me shovel snow off the driveway. She was four years old. By herself, she had put on everything she could to stay warm and dry (imagine Ralphie's little brother in *A Christmas Story*).

Meanwhile, I began to shovel the snow. But I had no idea that inside, my daughter was planning to do everything she could to help me. So she waddled out of the garage with a snow shovel that almost stood taller than she did and said, "Dad, I want to help you shovel the snow."

It's not about my greatness or your greatness, it's about the greatness of God. It's about the kindness of a God who would say, "I want to do this with you because I think it would be really great."

I really like shoveling snow. I value shoveling it perfectly and efficiently. I was thinking, *She's only going to slow me down. She's going to make my work harder.* I said rather dismissively, "Honey, I've got to do this myself. Just go back in." She dropped the shovel and sadly shuffled back inside the house.

Oh man, I felt awful because God's Spirit convicted me immediately. It was as if the Holy Spirit said to me, "Ashley, did you ever stop to think that *maybe she just wanted to be with you* and maybe, just maybe, that was more important than how effectively or efficiently you shoveled the driveway?"

A few years ago, God reminded me of that story when I was questioning my role as a sent person. He used that story of my daughter wanting to spend time with me to understand His perspective on my identity as a leader sent to reach graduate students with the gospel. I imagined God saying something like this: "Well, I really don't need you to save the grad students of the world, and I am pretty sure you are going to make My job a lot harder. But back in eternity past when I was thinking about how I might reach them and how I might use Cru to be a part of that work, I was wondering if you, Ashley, would really enjoy doing this with Me. I wondered how special it would be if you and I could go after this together."

Isn't that cool to consider? God doesn't need us. We might actually mess things up and make the work harder like a small child trying to shovel snow. But He wants to be with us. It's not about my greatness or your greatness, my ability or your ability, or however you feel about that. It's about the greatness of God. It's about the kindness of a God who would say, "I want to do this with you because I think it would be really great. I think it would be really fun. I think it would be really special that we get to do this together." Although we don't see God speaking like this in Scripture, I think it reflects His heart and character.

So think about the people in your life. Think about the people God has sovereignly placed you next to in your neighborhood, family, workplace, or school. Write your name in that story where God says, "You know, in eternity past I decided to reach this group of people and I thought that it would be fun to do this with you, [insert your name]." Isn't that great?

That's where our hope and courage come from. Our hope and courage don't come from our personality or gifting. Our hope and courage come from the reality that we have an awesome, incredible God who will save His people and who invites us to be a part of it with Him. God therefore uses us so we might enjoy being together, but also because it builds our faith and attaches us to an eternal purpose.

God is sending people. He is sending you. The most frequent way Jesus describes God the Father in the gospel of John is "the Father who sent me." Jesus knew exactly who He was, and we embrace this same sent identity when we remember what He said in John 20:21: "As the Father has sent me, I am sending you."

I am sending you.

Later in Romans 10:14–15, Paul also declares our sent identity as he describes *how the gospel spreads*. What is God's plan for the spreading of the gospel? *Sent people.* Remember what Paul writes:

> How, then, can they call on the one they have not believed in? And how can they believe in the one of whom they have not heard? And how can they hear without someone preaching to them? And how can anyone preach *unless they are sent*? As it is written: "How beautiful are the feet of those who bring good news!"

You don't have to wait to begin your sent life in light of these three core principles. God is sending you right now. In our very first class that we teach on living a sent life, we invite participants to think of five people God has placed in their lives. They write down those five people and commit to pray for them and to begin taking steps of faith to talk to them about Jesus. Which five people would you put on your own list? Pause a moment and pray, asking God to bring those five people to your mind as you read through this book.

Finally, if you think about it, the majority of people reading these words right now were brought into a relationship with Jesus *because God sent someone* into their lives to talk about Him. Who was that person for you? Can you now imagine being that person to someone else?

He sent others to you. Now, He sends you.

YOUR SENT LIFE

Consider / Discuss

1. Do you see evidence that *God is at work around you to draw people to Himself*? Make a list of people you know who already seem interested in spiritual things. If you don't see evidence that God is at work around you, pray that God shows you how He is working.

2. Why do you think *God chooses to use people* in His rescue mission instead of some other kind of way? Why does He invite us to cooperate with Him?

3. When you read the Great Commission, what do you feel? Guilt? Duty? Excitement? Fear? Write a few sentences about what Jesus' words that *invite us into the work of evangelism* stir up in you and why.

4. After reading this chapter, has your motivation to talk about Jesus changed? Why? If it hasn't, what would you need to know or feel that might motivate you to share the gospel with others?

Steps of Faith:

1. Begin praying for five people God has placed in your life who do not know Him. Ask the Lord to help you see how He is working in their lives.

2. To start your journey of talking openly about Jesus, write down a few sentences about what you most want people to know about Him.

3. As your first faith step, consider asking someone in your life who doesn't yet know Jesus this question: "Have you ever felt that God is working in your life? What was that like?" Maybe this person will then ask you if you've ever experienced God working in your life. What would you say?

4. Who did God send to help you begin a relationship with Jesus? Consider writing a thank-you note or reaching out in some other way to honor that person.

CHAPTER 2

Believing the Gospel

I am not ashamed of the gospel . . .

—Romans 1:16

Several years ago, I (Ashley) hung up the phone knowing that I had just finished a conversation that would change my ministry —and life—forever. I had called my good friend and mentor Randy Newman because I was stuck in helping the graduate students I mentored to more fully embrace sharing the gospel with their friends. I was able to effectively give our students the "how-to" of sharing their faith. However, I struggled in giving our students the "want-to" of sharing their faith.

They knew what to do. They knew that they should be doing it. They just didn't *want* to.

Or more accurately, their desire wasn't strong enough to overcome all the barriers to tell others about Jesus. And to be honest, I too struggled with the same thing—and I was in full-time ministry!

Randy helped me see that our "want-to" was meant to be cultivated by two sides of the same coin. One side depicts the greatness of Jesus and the gospel. The other side pictures the lostness of people apart from Christ. We really need both. We can't have one without the other. Focusing only on the greatness of Jesus and the gospel could lead us to just celebrating among ourselves as Christians and staying within our Christian circles or holy huddle, as some have called it. Dwelling only on the lostness of people apart from Christ likely would lead to despair or simply giving up.

But when we put them together, we get to see what Rick Hove, the National Director of Cru's ministry to professors, calls the Great Collision. In the Great Collision, God's undeserved mercy (the greatness of Jesus and the gospel) collides with people's formerly unrealized need (their lostness apart from Christ). And we realize that as *sent ones*, we don't just get a front-row seat to watching the Great Collision happen in others' lives; we get to be a part of it all.

On our call, Randy continued to explain that these two gospel convictions—the greatness of Jesus and the gospel, and the lostness of people apart from Christ—aren't instantly fully formed in us. They have to be cultivated. In other words, the more we grow in understanding and embracing these gospel convictions, the more our "want-to" will grow. So, how does this happen? As sent people, how do we cultivate these gospel convictions and thus the "want-to"?

First of all, let me say that this is a work both of God and of us. We have to cooperate—for sure—*and* it's a supernatural work that God's Spirit needs to accomplish in us. We don't have the power in ourselves to cultivate these convictions. Neither can we effectively be guilted or shamed into embracing them more. The apostle Paul commands us, "Do not conform to the pattern of this world, but be transformed by the renewing of your mind" (Rom. 12:2). As we allow the Holy Spirit to renew our minds regarding these gospel convictions—alongside the three core principles—He will transform us into *sent ones* with greater and greater "want-to."

Specifically, we are cooperating with the Holy Spirit to build these convictions in our life by continually asking and answering the following two questions:

1. Do I really believe that the gospel is good news?
2. Do I really believe that every person is lost apart from Christ?

Do I really believe that the gospel is good news?

As a Christian, I (Ashley) do absolutely believe theologically that the gospel is good news. I completely affirm Paul's declaration in his letter to the church in Rome (Rom. 1:16–17):

> For I am not ashamed of the gospel, because it is the power of God that brings salvation to everyone who believes: first to the Jew, then to the Gentile. For in the gospel the righteousness of God is revealed—a righteousness that is by faith from first to last, just as it is written: "The righteous will live by faith."

I am not and was not ashamed of the gospel, but at times I acted as if I were. When I imagined talking with others about the gospel, I didn't always think of the gospel as *good* news. Instead, I was prone to think of it primarily as *uncomfortable* news, or as *awkward* news, or as *weird* news, or even as *judgmental,* or *bad,* news. I was permitting the world and my own unrenewed mind—instead of God and the authority of His word—to characterize the gospel.

But hear the gospel again and be reminded that it really is *good* news. The gospel tells us that the God of the universe created us and that He created us to be perfectly loved by Him and to know Him personally. That's *good* news! And did you know that Christianity and Judaism are the only two religions of the world that teach that the God of the universe can be known personally? No other religion does.

The gospel tells us that we are broken and sinful; the gospel teaches that by active rebellion and/or by passive indifference we reject God. It tells us that there are eternal consequences for our sin. We are separated from His love and from knowing Him personally, and we face an eternity in hell separated from God, His love, and His goodness and instead experience His wrath. Furthermore, the gospel tells us that *we are absolutely incapable of fixing this and saving ourselves.* Now, this doesn't feel like good news, but consider the alternative. What if God never told us what our problem was? No one wants to get a cancer diagnosis. But what if they did have cancer and no one ever diagnosed it for them?

The gospel tells us that God can and did offer the solution. God's Son, Jesus, came to earth as a man, lived a perfect life, took our sin onto Himself, died on the cross to pay the penalty of our sin, satisfied God's wrath, and raised Himself from the dead conquering both sin and the grave. Did you read that too quickly because it's become too familiar? Read the paragraph again and savor these truths.

That's *good* news!

The gospel tells us that we don't have to earn our way to God. We can't. Instead, the gospel tells us that we simply need to believe and trust. We need to believe and trust in the person and life of Christ, in His atoning work on the cross and in His resurrection from the dead. And we need to receive Christ into our lives by surrendering to Him as our Savior and Lord. That's *good* news!

Finally, the gospel tells us that God is making all things new. He is not only redeeming and restoring people. He is also at work to redeem and restore all of creation. One day everything will be as it was always intended to be. That's *good* news!

So, hopefully right now, having just heard the gospel again, you are affirming again, "Yes, I really believe that the gospel is *good* news!" But what about next week or next year? How can we keep asking this question and cultivating this gospel conviction so that our heart and mind affirm the goodness of the gospel to an even greater and deeper level? Good question. We will get to that momentarily. But first, let's take a look at the second question—the question pertaining to the other side of Randy's coin.

Do I really believe that every person is lost apart from Christ?

As a Christian, I also absolutely believe theologically that every person is lost apart from Christ. I affirm and take Jesus at His word when He described how He saw the people He ministered to. The apostle Matthew recorded, "When he saw the crowds, he had compassion on them, because they were harassed and helpless, like sheep without a shepherd" (Matt. 9:36). Isaiah said about himself and others, "Woe is me! For I am *lost*; for I am a man of unclean lips, and I dwell in the midst of a people of unclean lips; for my eyes have seen the King, the LORD of hosts!" (Isa. 6:5 ESV). Paul describes who we were apart from Christ in three powerful passages in Ephesians. First, consider:

> As for you, you were dead in your transgressions and sins, in
> which you used to live when you followed the ways of this

world and of the ruler of the kingdom of the air, the spirit
who is now at work in those who are disobedient. All of us
also lived among them at one time, gratifying the cravings of
our flesh and following its desires and thoughts. Like the rest,
we were by nature deserving of wrath. (2:1–3)

Paul tells us that apart from Christ, we are spiritually dead and
deserving of wrath. Next, Paul invites readers then and now to "remember that you were at that time separated from Christ, alien-
ated from the commonwealth of Israel and strangers to the cov-
enants of promise, having no hope and without God in the world"
(2:12 ESV). Finally in Ephesians 4:18–19, Paul writes of those not
knowing Jesus:

> They are darkened in their understanding, alienated from
> the life of God because of the ignorance that is in them,
> due to their hardness of heart. They have become callous
> and have given themselves up to sensuality, greedy to practice
> every kind of impurity. (ESV)

Again, I truly affirm these verses and the others in Scripture that
tell us that every person is lost apart from Christ. I understand
we are spiritually dead apart from Christ, under God's wrath, and
without hope. But do I really believe it? Do I allow these truths to
shape how I see others? Do I see others the same way God does?
He sees them as fearfully and wonderfully made (Ps. 139:14) who
at this time live within His providential care and common grace
(Matt. 5:45), but *He sees them as lost*—lost men and women that
stir His heart with great compassion.

At times, I do see people the way God sees them. But at other times, I don't. Instead, I see them as doing fine, certainly a lot better than most other people in the world. If they are struggling, I am concerned for them during that season, but I can too quickly think of the old adage "this too shall pass" and fail to see them as ones with needs that will not pass unless God breaks into their life.

> *Some people I see are doing really well. In many ways, their life seems better than my own. I can even be tempted with the thought, "Maybe they don't need Jesus."*

Some people I see are doing really well. They seem happy. Things are working out for them. In many ways, their life seems better than my own. I can even be tempted with the thought, "Maybe *they* don't need Jesus." I vividly remember one day when God corrected my vision. I was chatting with one of my classmates. This was the guy in grad school who got everything right. He sailed through his classes. He loved his research. His experiments worked all the time. He is the only person I know who was having a truly easy time in grad school; he was brilliant, very gifted, naturally curious, and he worked hard. He was in a significant relationship with a young woman he had been dating for a long time. You get the picture. But he was also very disinterested in God—or seemingly so.

We struck up a conversation, and he asked me how I had spent the weekend. I shared that Heather and I attended church and participated in a class on marriage that was really helping us as an engaged couple. His whole countenance changed. He told me that he was struggling in his relationship with his girlfriend and would love a class like that. From that moment on, I saw him differently. I still saw all his gifts and strengths. But I also saw that he too had real needs and an interest in God that I had for the most part been blind to. By His Spirit, God helped me see my friend the way He saw him.

Perhaps the greatest reason I don't see people the way God sees them is that at times I am too distracted to even see them. Oh, I physically see them. We talk. But in the fast-paced, short attention span, distracted world we have created, we might not get beyond "How's the weather?" kind of conversations.

So, what do we do? Again, how can we keep asking ourselves, *Do I really believe that every person is lost apart from Christ?* and cultivate this gospel conviction so that we see others the way God sees them and move toward them with great compassion?

To keep asking and answering this question as well as the first one, Heather and I have adopted the following four practices. They have helped us grasp in deeper ways just how much we needed Jesus—and still do. The gospel and Jesus have become much more precious to us. We more regularly experience the power and impact of the gospel in our own lives. Through it all, we increasingly want those around us to also know the hope and power of the gospel. Our "want-to" grows.

1. Look for the gospel in every passage of Scripture you read and study.

The Bible is much more than a collection of stories and a list of dos and don'ts. All of Scripture is telling one story—the story of Jesus and our need for Him. As the *Jesus Storybook Bible* proclaims, "every story whispers His name."[1] Every passage in some way points us to Jesus and the gospel and/or our need for Him. So, when you read and study the Bible, look *for* the gospel every time. Then when you consider how to apply the Scripture to your life, look *to* the gospel every time. Run to Jesus, acknowledge that you can't follow Him in your own strength, and ask Him to empower and lead you by His Spirit to do so.

2. Regularly practice confession of sin to personally experience the gospel.

Confession involves simply acknowledging our sin to God, experiencing His forgiveness, and choosing to cooperate with the Lord as He cleanses us from all unrighteousness (1 John 1:9). At the heart of it all, confession says the same thing about our sin as God does. It goes beyond mere whitewashing or making less of our sin. True, heartfelt—and gospel-transforming—confession makes more of our sin by looking at the sin beneath the sin. It leads us to drill down into the broken values and idols we have set up against God. But confession doesn't stay there. It then compels us to see our need for Jesus in much greater ways. When this happens, the forgiveness we experience thrills our soul. Our hearts can't help but leap with gratitude to God for the hope of freedom from the sin and underlying brokenness that ensnare us.

3. Share stories of God's work in your life with one another.

As followers of Jesus, we are surrounded by many stories of God's supernatural work. Every believer you know is a walking miracle. No one comes to faith in Christ and experiences the transformation and life He alone gives apart from the supernatural intervening of God. No one. But do we know these stories? Share with one another how God rescued you and continues to work in your life in powerful ways. Don't hold back on the details and impact of all that God has done. Can you imagine how God could work in our hearts as we heard and told these stories? Heather will teach more about the power of these stories in chapter 9.

4. Seek to understand more fully those around you.

Likewise, we are surrounded by people who don't yet know Jesus. But God likely is working in ways we haven't seen or don't know of. I have rarely met someone who hasn't had some encounter with God at some point in their life. And everyone has a story and needs that only God can meet. Get to know them and their story. As you do, your heart for them and for the gospel will grow. We will talk more about practical ways to do this in chapters 6–8.

One final crucial note: As you seek to cultivate the two sides of the coin my friend Randy described and grow your "want-to," don't wait to talk with others about Jesus. All too often, we fail to "get in the game" because we are waiting for some level of maturity to do so. When we wait, we miss some incredible gospel opportunities, and we miss one of the best ways to grow our "want-to"—living out of our sent identity.

Yes, it's true. The more we cultivate these gospel convictions, the more we will live out of our sent identity. But catch this: the more we live out of our sent identity, the more we will cultivate these gospel convictions. By God's great design, they mutually reinforce one another.

I kept thinking, **Dude, why don't you put your drink down and go help your family?** *I thought about striking up a conversation, but I really didn't want to.*

I was reminded of this several months ago on a flight to Denver. Shortly after takeoff, the man sitting next to me ordered alcohol. He didn't even wait for the beverage service to begin. Shortly later, he ordered another drink. Meanwhile, his wife, young child, and another woman (presumably his or his wife's mother) sat a few rows behind us. His wife looked despondent and the other woman was trying to calm and comfort their child as best as she could. She was not succeeding.

I kept thinking, *Dude, why don't you put your drink down and go help your family?* I thought about striking up a conversation, but I really didn't want to. In fact, I was just trying not to get mad. My "want-to" wasn't there. The goodness of the gospel didn't move my heart in that moment. The man's need was there, but that didn't motivate me to action either. Instead, it overwhelmed me. And then something very curious happened.

The Holy Spirit reminded me of a recent conversation with Heather. Before my trip, Heather and I had begun mapping out this book and were talking a lot about our sent identity. Specifically, we talked of how God sends believers as an intervening presence into difficult situations. The Holy Spirit reminded me of that conversation and impressed upon me that this was one of those situations. He was sending me and would show me what to say and what to do.

So I asked the man where he was headed—the safest, easiest question you can ask someone flying—and he told me that he was headed to be with his wife's family because her dad had died unexpectedly just a few hours earlier. Her father was in his sixties and incredibly healthy and fit. However, he suffered a major heart attack and died instantly. My seatmate told me he had been up the entire night taking care of his stunned and heartbroken wife. They were on a plane headed to his wife's home and had no idea what they were going to face or what they were going to do when they got there.

Instantly, my heart softened. My "want-to" returned in full

measure. He and his family needed God to move in powerful ways. We talked a long time and I learned that he and his family were committed Christ followers. This man didn't need to meet Jesus. He just needed someone at that moment to point him back to Jesus. I answered questions. I encouraged him. I asked how I could pray. Through it all, I kept reminding him that God was with him and his family and would continue to be so in the coming days.

Isn't Jesus such a good shepherd? He leaves the ninety-nine to go after the one (Luke 15:4), and He uses us as a comforting and guiding presence on His behalf. The gospel really is good news. People truly are lost apart from Christ. Jesus grows our heart for them. And He sends us to them that they may come to Him and find rest for their souls (Matt. 11:28–29).

YOUR SENT LIFE

Consider / Discuss

1. What makes the gospel such good news? Explain in your own words the good news about knowing Jesus. What does He offer? Why do we need Him?

2. How do you connect with the words the Bible uses to explain our lives apart from Christ: lost, helpless, harassed, and spiritually dead? Where do you see evidence of people suffering like this around you?

3. Do you believe every person is lost and spiritually dead apart from Christ? Do you remember what your life was like before knowing Christ?

4. Why is the gospel good news for you personally? What did Jesus save you from?

Steps of Faith:

1. Begin the practice of preaching the gospel to yourself every morning. Where do you need forgiveness of sin and the power of the Holy Spirit today?

2. Make a list of people in your "crowd." Ask God to help you have compassion on them and see them as "harassed and helpless, like sheep without a shepherd" (Matt. 9:36). These may be the same people on your list from chapter 1.

3. Begin praying for the five people on your list. Pray that they would sense their need for God. Also pray blessing over their lives today.

4. What stories would you share with others about God's work in your life to help connect you again to the good news of the gospel? Begin writing down a few key times in your life when you believed God was rescuing you.

CHAPTER 3

Believing God's Titles and Job Descriptions for Your Life

Christian disciples are sent men and women—sent out in the same work of world evangelism to which the Lord was sent, and for which he gave his life. Evangelism is not an optional accessory to our life. It is the heartbeat of all that we are called to be and do.

—Dr. Robert Coleman, *The Master Plan of Evangelism*

For twenty years, I (Heather) have been growing into the truth of Robert Coleman's words above that I'm a *sent* person, and that this sent designation forms the crux of all I am "called to be and do." Ashley and I learned to ground our marriage in the three core principles (see chapter 1), and we reaffirm the good news of the gospel and the lostness of people without Jesus.

But this year in my journey to understand my "sent" identity, I realized that the Lord also provides four powerful titles that serve as metaphors to help us understand who we are in Christ even more fully. But before we dive into those four, let's explore the images and feelings you might associate with the key description that precedes them.

We are *sent*.

Jesus, most of all, saw Himself as *sent* by the Father. And He lived a sent life.

He explains to His disciples in John 6:38: "For I have come down from heaven not to do my will but to do the will of him who sent me." A few chapters earlier in John 4:34, Jesus tells us that His food—His sustenance in life—is "to do the will of him who sent me and to finish his work."

When you think of that verb *sent*, what comes to mind? In the most immediate and obvious way, you most likely see someone dispatched on a mission. When someone sends you, the action involves *a strategic location with a specific assignment.* Just as the Father sends Jesus to a precise location in the ancient world, we too live sent lives in the location God chooses for us. But does God really choose our location? Consider Acts 17:24–28 where Paul tells us something wonderful about where we live:

> The God who made the world and everything in it is the Lord of heaven and earth and does not live in temples built by human hands. And he is not served by human hands, as if he needed anything. Rather, he himself gives everyone life and breath and everything else. From one man he made all the nations, that they should inhabit the whole earth; and he marked out their appointed times in history and the boundaries of their lands. God did this so that they would seek him and perhaps reach out for him and find him, though he is not far from any one of us. "For in him we live and move and have our being."

This passage indicates that God sets the times and places where people live, including us today. Many readers overlook the reason why: "God did this so that [people] would seek him and perhaps reach out for him and find him." People seek the Lord and find Him where believers are present because God exists within us as we are indwelt by the Holy Spirit. People reach out for God and meet Him *through us*. When I couple Paul's words in Acts 17 with the truth of God's sovereignty to choose where I live, I remember how in Daniel 5:23b, we're told we serve a God who holds our life and all our ways in His hands. If that seems too specific and impossible for God to know and care where our apartment sits or where in the neighborhood you live, remember Psalm 33:15 and how God "forms the hearts of all" and "considers everything they do." God indeed sends us to a chosen location. And here, we know that God is at work, and He chooses to use us right where we are.

As you shape your life to the truth of God's leading you to a specific location, for a clear mission, extraordinary things will begin happening to you. Several years ago, it was as if God delivered clear deployment papers to my heart when I transitioned to a new life in Centre County, Pennsylvania:

Love the people *here.*

Become available to the people *here.*

Tell people about Jesus *here.*

Living on my street wasn't an accident. Living near these neighbors wasn't an accident. As a sent person, I wished to make myself available to love the people right around me and to introduce them to Jesus. I canceled appointments that took me away from the neighborhood, and I decided I would spend more time near my home.

One Tuesday morning, I sat on my old couch with a cup of coffee and told my husband I was staying home all day to "be available to my neighbors." This was my new sent life. I spent the morning praying about my sent calling. I wondered what would happen as the hours passed and my coffee cup emptied. Was this commitment to stay available wrong or even crazy?

Just as I was about to abandon my mission, I heard the crunch of tires on the driveway, and a neighbor I didn't know very well stepped out of her minivan. As she balanced two cups of coffee in her hands, she walked up to the doorway and rang the doorbell with her elbow. When I answered the door, she said, "I just got a new haircut, and I wanted to show someone. I have coffee. Are you available?"

We spent the rest of the morning together. She became one of my dearest friends, and I journeyed alongside her for a decade as she began seeking for God and trusting Him. (In fact, years later, this same woman called me to tell me when it was time to tell another friend about Jesus.) That day, I knew I had been deployed to a location.

Within five years, my neighborhood became the site of so many spiritual conversations, decisions for Christ, baptisms, and Bible studies that all flowed from believing God had chosen me to live where I was for the purpose of introducing people to Jesus. We hosted Saturday Morning Pancakes for families to come in their pajamas with their children that led to an investigative Bible study of the book of John. We organized a Walk-to-School campaign and a Neighborhood Fitness Group that drew up to fifty neighbors that led to invitations to church, spiritual conversations, and deep friendships that continue to this day.

Every day in my neighborhood and workplace, I now have the expectation that God is *sending me to someone* who needs to hear about Him. I've now learned to think of every interaction as a divine appointment. Every encounter is a possible rescue mission on my deployment. It makes my workday and home life adventurous and filled with intimacy with Jesus. I often unpack my bag at work and whisper to Jesus, "Who will it be today, Lord? Who are You sending me to?"

Think about your home. Think about your larger community. Think about your place of work. Think about your natural pathways of errand running, gym, volunteer work, or any other place you find yourself most days. Now consider the truth: It's no accident where you live and where you spend your time. God sent you there because someone there needs to know Jesus.

As if our short word "sent" weren't enough to provide what we needed to begin a fresh day with the Lord, the Bible also offers four beautiful, compelling, and helpful metaphors that flesh out the sent identity. In the New Testament, we discover these titles that correspond to our various roles as sent people: *Farmer, Fisherman, Ambassador,* and *Royal Priest.* These descriptions in the Bible aren't literal—meaning they serve as useful comparisons and images to help us understand in a figurative sense who we are. But they hold immense power. I love these metaphors because they help me as I enter any new setting.

The titles of *farmer, fisherman, ambassador,* and *royal priest* come with various actions—or job descriptions—that help us understand our roles better.

As we build up a fresh identity of who we are and what we do as followers of Christ, we find that we enter a room with purpose, authority, and vision for how to engage people. Since evangelism is often more a matter of confidence rather than training, these metaphors embolden us to move into biblical roles.

A group of students recently asked me why God gives so many different metaphors for our sent identity. Is it because they appeal to different personalities? Is it because God knew each role would matter in different contexts? I cannot know for sure, but I like to think God wanted us to have as many access points to our sent identity as possible.

Titles	Job Descriptions
Hardworking Farmer	*Sows, Plows, Plants, Harvests*
Patient Fisherman	*Baits, Casts, Catches*
Confident Ambassador	*Represents, Delivers Message, Informs*
Authoritative Royal Priest	*Blesses, Teaches God's Word*

The Hardworking Farmer
"A farmer went out to sow his seed . . ." Matthew 13:3

When I began to understand my sent identity in those years as a graduate student at the University of Michigan, the first metaphor God used in my life was that of a *farmer*. I noticed this phrase "hardworking farmer" (2 Tim. 2:6) and then how Paul in particular describes our work in the world as sowing "spiritual seed" (1 Cor. 9:11). In fact, there's quite a bit of sowing, planting, and reaping imagery in Scripture.

Paul describes God as the one who supplies "seed to the sower" to "increase your store of seed [to] enlarge the harvest of your righteousness" (2 Cor. 9:10). Paul also encourages us to "sow generously" so we might "reap generously" of a spiritual harvest of souls (2 Cor. 9:6). I had never seen myself as a farmer before. What did I know of farming? I'm a military daughter and a city girl. I did know this: when I think of a farmer, I picture hard work, soil, and seeds.

Consider the story in Luke 8:4–8 where we encounter Jesus teaching about a farmer:

> While a large crowd was gathering and people were coming to Jesus from town after town, he told this parable: "A farmer went out to sow his seed. As he was scattering the seed, some fell along the path; it was trampled on, and the birds ate it up. Some fell on rocky ground, and when it came up, the plants withered because they had no moisture. Other seed fell among thorns, which grew up with it and choked the plants. Still other seed fell on good soil. It came up and yielded a crop, a hundred times more than was sown."

And then Jesus explains His parable in Luke 8:11–15:

> "This is the meaning of the parable: The seed is the word of God. Those along the path are the ones who hear, and then the devil comes and takes away the word from their hearts, so that they may not believe and be saved. Those on the rocky ground are the ones who receive the word with joy when they hear it, but they have no root. They believe for a while, but in the time of testing they fall away. The seed that fell among thorns stands for those who hear, but as they go on their way they are choked by life's worries, riches and pleasures, and they do not mature. But the seed on good soil stands for those with a noble and good heart, who hear the word, retain it, and by persevering produce a crop."

This parable instructs us what the good soil of a person's heart looks like and how to cultivate it. We find four kinds of soil: *shallow soil, rocky soil, thorny soil,* and *good soil.* When I think of my sent work as a farmer, it's a metaphor not only for planting seeds of the gospel, but also for preparation *before* planting the seed of the gospel.

The hardworking farmer prepares the soil of a person's heart—adding depth to shallow understanding, removing the rocks of disbelief, cynicism, or a worldview that cannot support Christianity, and weeding to expose the damage and idolatry of worries, riches, and pleasure. I think about the farmer when I read Jeremiah 4:3 when God says to the people, "Break up your unplowed ground and do not sow among thorns," or in Hosea 10:12 when the prophet writes, "Sow righteousness for yourselves, reap the fruit of unfailing love, and break up your unplowed ground; for it is time to seek the LORD, until he comes and showers his righteousness on you." I think of what it means to "break up unplowed ground" for others around me.

While not explicitly presenting a gospel message, this farming role prepares those around us for when someone does present the invitation to know God personally.

When engaging with others, the hardworking farmer asks, "What kind of soil am I dealing with here? What can I do to make this heart more ready to hear about Jesus?"

I consider how the very language I use in my workplace, my acts of service, and my intentional attitude of praise could help create the conditions in a person's heart so they would *want* to know Jesus, where the gospel *could* be true, and where a life of joy and hope *would* become a possibility. For example, if a student or colleague has never imagined spiritual realities, and I speak about the soul, heaven, angels, eternity, or answered prayer, I'm creating a world—a landscape in the soul—in which spiritual things *could be true*. I'm making good soil. The hardworking farmer understands his or her sent role as first preparing the soil that helps give people a context for understanding the gospel.

As an instructor at Penn State, sharing my authentic Christian life with students—outside of class or before class begins, or when questions arise in the context of class discussion—is an important part of my work and teaching philosophy. Students learn what I value and how I live my life, just as I learn about their lives and the values that shape their choices. I never force spiritual conversations or make students feel uncomfortable expressing their own faith traditions. Over the past decade, I've been praised by the administration for appropriately modeling a religious life for students, for praying for students and caring about their lives, and for being available to connect students to religious organizations on campus. I understand, too, that I'm free to express my faith in Jesus as part of the free-speech constitutional protections afforded to all professors on campus. In fact, you can read more about the influence and practice of Christian professors in a book I edited called *A Grander Story: An Invitation to Christian Professors.*[1]

The words I speak about my spiritual life flow naturally from who I am and my role as a spiritual farmer. A spiritual farmer would consider Philippians 4:8 and the call to think about and speak about whatever is true, noble, right, pure, lovely, admirable, excellent, and praiseworthy. According to Paul in Philippians 2:14–15 when we do "everything without grumbling or arguing," we "shine among them like stars in the sky." I ask myself if my words, attitude, and behavior help cultivate the soil of a person's heart, or plant weeds and toss rocks by negativity, cynicism, or doubt. I don't want to do anything to harm the soil of a person's soul.

While not explicitly presenting a gospel message, this farming role prepares those around us for when someone does present the invitation to know God personally. That person might be you, but often, God may send another person to talk about Jesus and enjoy the spiritual harvest that you helped cultivate. I like to remember that the hardworking farmer prepares the soil, breaking apart the hard, dry places of the heart to receive the seed when it comes. As Paul describes his own ministry in 1 Corinthians 3:6–7, he may have planted the actual seed of the gospel, but others were at work to water. Behind every kind of service, however, God is the one "who makes things grow" (7).

Finally, I remember that a farmer *sows the seed* which is the Word of God. That's what all the plowing is for. Without the seed, all that labor is literally fruitless. I wanted to sow seed, but I didn't know how to "sow the word." I didn't know God's Word well enough to share with others. When I began to study and memorize Scripture to use it naturally in conversation and to apply it aptly in any situation, I found myself amazed at the results. Speaking Scripture into a conversation not only opened doors for full gospel presentations, but this practice also helped me quickly identify how a person felt about God and their own spiritual lives. It's a skill I continue to cultivate in my farming role. In any conversation, a farmer asks, "How can I apply a passage of Scripture to this situation? Is there something I might share from the Bible to plant a seed into the heart of this person?" Recently, I talked about what God was teaching me about overcoming fear and anxiety when I realized how stressed out two of my colleagues were. I shared a passage of Scripture (2 Tim. 1:7 about not having a "spirit of fear"), and both colleagues immediately stopped to ask me more about what the Bible says about fear and stress. One professor said, "How do you get rid of that spirit of fear? Whatever that is, I think I have that!" This question opened the door to talk about Jesus and His power over our fear.

During the day, I think of how I might finish this sentence: "What you're saying reminds me of something I read in the Bible where God says _____." Each time I've been able to do this, a spiritual conversation began. However, when I train others about this part of our sent identity, they inevitably feel ill-equipped. My best advice for those feeling this way is to simply start writing down Bible verses that the Lord has used in your life, commit them to memory, and practice speaking them with your family and friends. Even if you only know three or four passages of Scripture, imagine sowing these into a conversation.

You might even tell your coworkers that you're trying to accomplish a new goal of memorizing encouraging words from the Bible. You might say, "I'm working on a new skill of Bible memorization. May I share a verse I'm working on?" You can do it! Think of yourself as a farmer going out to sow the Word, and enter the spaces of your life with that mindset. And remember you're not alone. We are working together. We are the body of Christ together in this harvest field. Jesus refers to our roles as farmers together in John 4:35–38:

> "Don't you have a saying, 'It's still four months until harvest'? I tell you, open your eyes and look at the fields! They are ripe for harvest. Even now the one who reaps draws a wage and harvests a crop for eternal life, so that the sower and the reaper may be glad together. Thus the saying 'One sows and

another reaps' is true. I sent you to reap what you have not worked for. Others have done the hard work, and you have reaped the benefits of their labor."

We are farmers together—some of us are preparing the soil, some are planting, and some are harvesting—but what matters most is that God *is doing this work now*. In fact, in your role as a spiritual farmer, you might find yourself doing any of these tasks.

The call to open our eyes and look at the fields, in fact, inspired Ashley to name our evangelism training course "Look Up" to invite others to see the harvest of people around them. As you will read in a later chapter on sharing the gospel message and inviting a response, you'll feel more empowered in your role as a farmer poised before a great harvest. But meanwhile, we might enter any new setting and embrace our roles as hardworking farmers who prepare the soil of a heart and sow the Word of God wherever we go.

The Patient Fisherman
"Come, follow me," Jesus said, "and I will send you out to fish for people." Matthew 4:19

The second metaphor God uses in Scripture to flesh out our sent identity involves the *fisherman*. Jesus invites us to follow Him and He will make us *fish for people*. I recently read a report from the Barna group that 38 percent of practicing Christians say they have no non-Christian friends or family members.[2] This means they are fishermen who aren't anywhere near the fish. When people ask me why I'm able to have so many conversations about Jesus with people who don't know Him, I tell them it's because I hang out with a lot of people who don't yet know Jesus. I intentionally go where the fish are. In fact, whenever I find myself comfortable with my church activities—the potlucks, Bible studies, women's events, and all gatherings of various kinds—the Lord reminds me that I'm a sent one. I can't stay at church all week. I need to go to where the fish are. More and more, I ask myself where people gather who don't know Jesus, and I pray that God helps me get there.

Sent people go where the fish are.

And then they fish. They fish with *bait*. Of course I'm not talking about the negative connotation of "baiting" people using gimmicks or sneaking in spiritual conversation unnaturally. What is bait for someone fishing for people who need Christ? It's *spiritual language* that invites people to participate in a spiritual conversation about spiritual realities. If God is working in that person's life, I find they want to talk more. They ask about the concept I've brought up in natural conversation. If I'm teaching or interacting with colleagues in the English department or even relaxing in my neighborhood, I've learned to cast spiritual bait. I see myself as fishing for people. The bait takes the shape of key words that connect us to spiritual realities. Consider, for example, this list of ten simple spiritual words you might weave in conversation:

> *prayer, God, Jesus, blessing, church, peace,*
> *supernatural, Scripture, faith, spiritual*

When I'm with someone who doesn't know Jesus, I'll often talk naturally in conversation about how God recently answered a prayer. As I shared that sentence with my dental hygienist (chapter 1), remember how she asked, "You pray? You pray to God?" The words "prayer" and "God" paved the way for a gospel conversation.

Likewise, you might mention in any situation or dilemma about how Jesus might respond. I spoke to the faculty in my seminar recently about how Jesus is a model for great teaching when you see Him wash the feet of the disciples. He's a servant most of all. This comment positioned me as a Christian to my colleagues and also gave them the opportunity to ask more about Jesus as a great teacher.

I also love saying joyful phrases about praying blessing over my children and even asking others if I can pray a blessing over them. Nobody has ever said, "No! I don't want a blessing." With students, I might begin a conversation describing some supernatural element in a movie or novel and then ask them if they've ever personally experienced some kind of supernatural event.

My favorite three words that cast bait for people include *Scripture*, *faith*, and *spiritual*. Recently, I simply described myself as someone on a spiritual journey, and the person immediately opened up to me. I asked, "Do you consider yourself as someone on a spiritual journey?" When she began crying, I said, "Can I share with you when my spiritual journey began with Jesus and what it's like today?" She wanted to hear more and more. I also love simply saying, "I read the coolest thing in Scripture." Sometimes people may ask what I mean by "Scripture." I've never had anyone tell me they didn't want to hear the cool thing I learned.

When it comes to regularly using spiritual language, don't be surprised if something amazing happens. A businesswoman I was introduced to awhile back invited me out to lunch. She was sensing the presence of what she called "something" in her life—something spiritual, but she didn't know how to describe what was happening or understand it. She didn't have the right language. She knew I was a Christian who wrote Christian books and regularly spoke about God, so she was eager to talk to someone about what she was experiencing.

We were seated at the restaurant at a corner table, away from the hubbub of the noontime crowd. Once we had placed our order, my new friend pulled out a notebook and pen as if to interview me. I prayed to the Lord and asked Him to give me all the right words to say. Her first question was about a single word I used all the time: *God.* She asked, "What do you mean when you say God? Who is God?"

I was able to answer her. I had cast the bait, and she was biting. I said, "I mean Jesus—the incarnation of God the Father—who indwells us by the Holy Spirit. I mean the triune God of Father, Son, and Holy Spirit." As we talked, I wanted her to know that Jesus was the living God, the exact representation of God's being from Colossians 1 to distinguish God from any other religion she might have encountered.

We talked about why it was right to worship Jesus, and I quoted Philippians 2:10–11 and how "at the name of Jesus every knee should bow . . . and every tongue acknowledge that Jesus Christ is Lord, to the glory of God the Father." She listened carefully and took notes on the language I was using. Then, she said this: "It feels like something is happening inside of me when I think about God. Is that strange how I think about God more inside of me and less outside of me? Do Christians think God is outside of them or inside of them?"

I responded, "Both!" It's actually very biblical to think that. In fact, when Jesus ascended into heaven, He said that it was good for Him to go away because He would send the Counselor, the Holy Spirit, who would dwell with us forever. I told her that when a person prays to receive Christ, God comes to live inside of us by the Holy Spirit.

She had never heard this before. She didn't understand that this is what Christians believe. Nobody had ever explained to her about the indwelling of Christ inside of us that enables us to have a conscious union with God. Her eyes began to fill with tears. She waited to speak again until our server had refilled our glasses.

She then said, "Well, I am feeling so many wonderful things are happening to me, and it feels like I'm on this spiritual journey, but I haven't done one thing to welcome it. I haven't done anything. Why is this happening? Why would this happen to me when I haven't done anything to deserve it?"

"Well," I said, "that sounds just like the word *grace*." I explained that this is God's grace that she cannot do anything to earn the favor of God; He pursues us even when we are far from Him.

"I have another question," she said eagerly. "Why am I so drawn to the concept of hope? Tell me about this spiritual word *hope*."

I explained that in Romans 15:13 that we learn that God is called a *God of hope*. Hope comes from Him. We continued to talk through our meal, through dessert, and then over coffee long after the lunch crowd had thinned out. We talked about the goodness of God, about Jesus, about answered prayer, and about living under the blessing of God. She ended our conversation by saying, "Well, I'm going to try all this."

I said, "Do you mean you want to open your heart to God?" She nodded. She had tears in her eyes. Later that evening at home, I considered how, whenever I feel like God made a mistake in sending me to my community, I would remember this woman who wanted to know more about spiritual words.

When I leave my home, I think of fishing. I will cast the bait of spiritual language and see who responds. And when I think of that adjective that the fisherman is "patient," I remember that sometimes I wait for years—sometimes decades—until a person wishes to engage in a spiritual conversation. This never discourages me. A good fisherman casts bait and waits patiently.

The Confident Ambassador
"We are therefore Christ's ambassadors, as though God were making his appeal through us." 2 Corinthians 5:20

The most exciting and comforting metaphor I next understood in Scripture was the *ambassador*. This title sounds oh so official and dignified, but it also removes the pressure from someone trying to drum up original ideas or personal opinions about Jesus.

Ambassadors come from their sending country—their true home—to serve as a representative to their host country. *They don't share their own opinion or viewpoints but rather only those of their country's leader.* The biblical ambassador comes with a message of reconciliation between his or her heavenly kingdom and the world we now live in. It's a beautiful metaphor for who we are in Christ. He leaves us on earth as delegates from our true home to bring this reconciliation about.

As a graduate student, the idea of walking into the English department as an ambassador for Christ thrilled me. And as I studied 2 Corinthians 5:11–21, I noted this word "ambassador" and this new mission called "the ministry of reconciliation." Paul writes,

> Since, then, we know what it is to fear the Lord, we try to persuade others. What we are is plain to God, and I hope it is also plain to your conscience…If we are "out of our mind," as some say, it is for God; if we are in our right mind, it is for you. For Christ's love compels us, because we are convinced that one died for all, and therefore all died. And he died

for all, that those who live should no longer live for themselves but for him who died for them and was raised again.

So from now on we regard no one from a worldly point of view. Though we once regarded Christ in this way, we do so no longer. Therefore, if anyone is in Christ, the new creation has come: The old has gone, the new is here! All this is from God, who reconciled us to himself through Christ and gave us the ministry of reconciliation: that God was reconciling the world to himself in Christ, not counting people's sins against them. And he has committed to us the message of reconciliation. We are therefore Christ's ambassadors, as though God were making his appeal through us. We implore you on Christ's behalf: Be reconciled to God. God made him who had no sin to be sin for us, so that in him we might become the righteousness of God.

The Lord used these eleven verses to change nearly everything about my attitude and mission in my workplace, neighborhood, and even in my home. Paul says that we live in these five ways that shifted my perspective: *we try to persuade others; we aren't concerned if people think we are out of our minds; God's love compels us; we've been given a ministry; God is making an appeal through us.*

Of course, I didn't understand fully what an ambassador did, but as I took notes on the ambassador role, I became excited. In the simplest sense of the biblical word, an ambassador is someone appointed by God to declare His will.[3] An ambassador communicates the message of the sending King, not his or her own original message.

Charles Spurgeon, in a sermon titled "God Beseeching Sinners by His Ministers," says it like this: "You see, we have nothing to tell you but what God has told us. We have not to stand in our pulpits, and utter original ideas, or to invent a gospel for you. No, we are simply the bearers of a message which God would have us deliver to you."[4] More recently, Francis Frangipane in his book *Spiritual Discernment and the Mind of Christ* writes this:

> We are called as "ambassadors for Christ" (2 Cor. 5:20; Eph. 6:20). A true ambassador not only represents his or her ruler; an ambassador knows that ruler's policies and how he thinks. He receives regular instruction and thus is current on the leader's goals. Should the ambassador be ignorant of the ruler's view, he does not offer his own opinions; he waits to hear from the one he represents. There are seven billion opinions in the world; the nations are not pining for our opinions, but to hear the words of the One we represent.[5]

When I read Frangipane's words, I'm challenged to know my Bible so well that I understand God's message for us. I want to present the truth of Scripture and so be freed up from spouting my own opinions on any matter. In fact, when I feel overwhelmed by a question from a colleague or neighbor about something controversial in society, I say, "I'm not telling you my opinion. My thoughts on this issue actually aren't what matters. It's what God has said. If anything, you can take issue with God and the Bible." The confidence I have as an ambassador matters because it means I enter into spaces understanding the authority of God's Word and the message God has instructed His ambassadors to give. I'm not worried about presenting my own ideas.

I recently arranged to meet with a friend who struggled with existential questions including mortality, whether God exists, and what it meant to experience God through nature. I arrived to our meeting prepared with a booklet to present the gospel, Bible verses about the immortality of our souls, the existence of God, and how we experience God through Jesus Christ and the gift of the Holy Spirit. While nature reflects the character of God as Creator and Sustainer, I knew I'd have to speak clearly about God as separate from nature and not *in* nature.

> *We don't need to lose heart or feel like anything depends on us. Instead, we set "forth the truth plainly" and let God handle the rest.*

But I was nervous. I didn't want her to feel pressured, angry, or condemned by me even though I knew she had been exploring New Age pathways and had come to believe that every religion had truth and a way to God. As I prayed about what to share with her and how to speak, my husband reminded me to speak *clearly, simply,* and *honestly.* He told me to tell her the truth about her soul, about Jesus, and about what it means to receive the free gift of salvation.

The Holy Spirit kept prompting me to read 2 Corinthians 4, which I believed would encourage my friend through a battle she was facing with her health. I knew she was losing heart, and this passage said so clearly in verses 16–18 these beautiful sentences:

> Therefore we do not lose heart. Though outwardly we are wasting away, yet inwardly we are being renewed day by day. For our light and momentary troubles are achieving for us an eternal glory that far outweighs them all. So we fix our eyes not on what is seen, but on what is unseen, since what is seen is temporary, but what is unseen is eternal.

I could share these verses with her and perhaps transition to talking eternity and our need for a savior.

But still, I was so nervous I felt sick. I was the one losing heart. I didn't feel smart enough or wise enough to talk to her. Thankfully, my eyes scanned the few verses above where God had a message for me, too, that reminded me of my ambassador role. Paul writes:

> Therefore, since through God's mercy we have this ministry, we do not lose heart. Rather, we have renounced secret and shameful ways; we do not use deception, nor do we distort the word of God. On the contrary, by setting forth the truth plainly we commend ourselves to everyone's conscience in the sight of God. And even if our gospel is veiled, it is veiled to those who are perishing. The god of this age has blinded the minds of unbelievers, so that they cannot see the light of the gospel that displays the glory of Christ, who is the image of God. For what we preach is not ourselves, but Jesus Christ as Lord, and ourselves as your servants for Jesus' sake. For God, who said, "Let light shine out of darkness," made his light shine in our hearts to give us the light of the knowledge of God's glory displayed in the face of Christ. (2 Cor. 4:1–6)

Notice what Paul writes to us here. We don't need to lose heart or feel like anything depends on us. Instead, we set "forth the truth plainly" and let God handle the rest. I wanted to make sure I presented Christ fully based on my own experience of Him, but Paul reminds us that "what we preach is not ourselves, but Jesus Christ..." At that moment, I knew God was asking me to step into my ambassador role; I would speak clearly and plainly about my King and deliver His message of salvation.

And I did! I first shared my own story, but then I talked about how someone comes to know Jesus. And while my friend continued to voice her objections, she shared her deep respect for me, her desire for prayer, and her wish to continue meeting.

I left our time together confident as an ambassador of the Lord. My plain speech did in fact "commend me" to her. I left our conversation exactly where I needed to: in the Lord's hands.

Finally, the ambassador title gives me confidence. I'm sent from the Lord with a message of reconciliation. When I doubt who I am, what my title is, or what I stand for, I remember the *confident ambassador*.

The Authoritative Royal Priest

"But you are a chosen people, a royal priesthood, a holy nation, God's special possession, that you may declare the praises of him who called you out of darkness into his wonderful light." 1 Peter 2:9

One day last semester, I had been reading about my role as a royal priest from 1 Peter 2:9 where Peter says I'm part of a "royal priesthood." I knew that a priest pronounced blessing and helped explain God's Word to people. I also knew the dominant picture of an Old Testament priest was someone entering the temple with the atoning sacrifice. I reasoned that I also enter spaces with the atoning sacrifice—Christ Jesus who indwells me by the Holy Spirit—and I'm making a way for others to know Him.

The title excited me. I thought about how "royal" was the highest designation in the Roman world, and to give someone the title of "priesthood" was the highest designation in the Jewish world. I therefore have been given the highest title available. In any setting,

I hold the highest title; this solved the problems of my insecurity or competition for my job title as I giggled when I sat in committee meetings when people asked me, "What's your title?"

I had been meditating on how the priests were always invited to "step forward and pronounce blessings in the name of the LORD" (Deut. 21:5) and how Levites would help explain God's Word to people as beautifully described in Nehemiah 8:8. We read this: "They read from the Book of the Law of God, making it clear and giving the meaning so that the people understood what was being read." When I considered my role as a *royal priest* from 1 Peter 2:9, I wondered if God had positioned me where I was to pronounce blessing and explain God's Word to others. I wanted to be that agent of blessing in people's lives that would lead me to introduce them to Jesus.

So again, I prayed. This time, I found myself on my knees in my hotel room in Texas where I had traveled for a Christian conference. I asked God to send me as a royal priest to bless others. "God," I cried, "would You send me forth as a royal priest to bless and minister Your name today? I'm available! I want to step forward and pronounce blessing!" I considered my life as I knelt on the hotel room floor. What did I have to offer? If I dug in my purse, I'd be more likely to find my list of a thousand vivid verbs than money. I thought about how I'm not rich in money to bless people, but I am rich in verbs and the desire to help others write. *Maybe God would send me forth to bless with verbs.* I knew God is always placing His people in strategic locations, so He could do something special right here in this hotel.

Rising from my knees, I traveled down to the lobby much earlier than I needed to arrive for breakfast, and I sat next to a friend who held the sign to direct folks to our conference prayer room.

Suddenly, a woman attending a medical conference in a different part of the hotel approached us. "I know I'm not part of your conference," she said, "but I saw the sign for prayer." Tears were falling from her eyes and dripping off of her chin.

I immediately asked how I could help. "What do you need, and how can I pray?"

And then, something extraordinary happened, something I won't ever forget.

The woman said this: "I was praying that God would send someone to help me learn how to write. I'm going to fail out of my graduate program unless I find someone who can teach me how to write like a graduate student." She asked if we could pray that God would send her help to learn to write at the graduate level.

The tears keep falling.

I held her by the hands with joy. "You need someone to help with writing? Someone who understands graduate students, who just happens to serve with Cru to help graduate students? Someone who teaches advanced writing? That's me! I'm the one! I have a list of a thousand vivid verbs! Jesus sent me here for you!"

We sat there marveling. I was an answer to her prayer; she was an answer to mine that God would send me forth to bless. We began a long-distance coaching relationship where I sent her my writing book, helped edit her material, and prayed for her journey as a graduate writer. How beautiful to think that God sent me to Texas from Pennsylvania for a woman who needed Him, and that He knew I'd pray in a hotel room that He might send me forth to bless with verbs.

As I've grown in my understanding of this title and job description to bless, I've taken seriously what it means to bless students for the last twenty years. God providentially chooses my students, and He does so because of people who need to know Him.

Believing I was a royal priest sent to a location of my classroom, I enact the same ritual every fresh semester. When I receive my new list of students and my classroom assignments, I find my way into my empty dark classrooms before the first day of class. I kneel down there and ask the Lord to consecrate the space for His purposes. I ask the Lord to bless the room and my teaching. Then, I touch every seat and imagine the student who will sit there.

I pray three things for that student, and sometimes I cry as I think about whoever will sit there. I pray that God would "turn [their] eyes from worthless things, and give [them] life in [His] word" (Ps. 119:37 NLT). I pray that God would give the student a deep sense of belonging in my classroom to combat the epidemic of loneliness on college campuses. Finally, I ask that things I do and say would plant seeds for the gospel (from my farming role).

I asked my officemate if I could pray a blessing over her job search. She said, "You know I'm an atheist, but yes! Please!"

This formal blessing of my students ends when I ask them if I can pronounce a blessing over them on the last day of class. Since many professors end their courses with statements of encouragement, wisdom giving, or quotations, I wanted to provide a famous written blessing. My Jewish students cry, "Yes!" since they are used to the tradition of being blessed. I often choose the traditional Irish Blessing, attributed to Saint Patrick, because of its rich Christian symbolism. As I read the Irish blessing over students, some of them begin to cry. I simply say this:

> May the road rise up to meet you.
> May the wind be always at your back.

May the sun shine warm upon your face;
the rains fall soft upon your fields and until we meet again,
may God hold you in the palm of His hand.[6]

During one semester as I prayed through my identity as a sent royal priest, I asked nearly everyone I encountered if I might pray a blessing over them. First, I passed a former student who I found out was being deployed to Afghanistan in the next week. I simply said, "May God bless you and protect you" and he was so grateful. Then, I asked my officemate if I could pray a blessing over her job search. She said, "You know I'm an atheist, but yes! Please!"

That same week, a former student from eight years prior came to my office with her boyfriend. They shyly peeked in the doorway. "Hello!" I called out, and after hugging her, I asked, "It's great to see you! Now, why are you here?"

As they took their seats, they explained that, together, they were headed overseas to take new jobs. They were filled with fear and anxiety about their new roles. As we talked about all the details of their adventure—locating an apartment, finding new friends, and establishing their adult lives abroad—I asked again, "Now why are you here?"

"Well," my former student stammered, "well, we are going away, and well, we don't really have anyone in our lives to send us off, I guess. We don't have anyone to . . ." she paused and looked awkwardly into her lap.

"You don't have anyone to give you their blessing?" She nodded eagerly. I said, "Would you like me to send you off with a blessing?"

"Oh, yes!" they both exclaimed, with faces now lit up.

"Then let me pray a blessing over you," I said with all the

authority of a true royal priest. I closed my office door. And because I wasn't sure if they were Christians, I prayed this blessing:

"Lord, we are here before You because of the shed blood of Jesus Christ on the cross who forgives our sins and enabled the way for us to come freely into Your presence in our time of need. Thank You that we simply confess our sins and by faith receive the free gift of salvation. Thank You that your Holy Spirit then guides and comforts us forever. I have here my friends who are traveling overseas. Lord, I ask You to pour out Your blessing on them. I pray that You bless their work, their search for friends, and their home there. Fill them with joy and peace as they travel and spread Your protection over them. Thank You that You are a loving God who cares for us. In Jesus' name, Amen."

They wiped tears from their eyes as I finished.

But my students coming to receive a blessing wasn't even the most powerful moment in my journey that semester of understanding my royal priest role.

In my classroom as I prayed for God to turn each student's eyes from worthless things, I had this one student—I'll call him Jack—who I felt especially drawn to pray for. He seemed like a stereotypical college student—someone who partied and who didn't want to be in class at all. But Jack kept coming to class earlier than the formal start time of my course to listen to me talk about my life. I would talk about my relationship to God, and in particular, that my husband and I didn't drink much alcohol. Jack couldn't believe it. He had recently turned twenty-one, which meant the opportunity to party more with his friends. The semester went on with Jack coming earlier and earlier and listening to anything I had to say about what I learned in church on Sunday or a Bible verse I liked. We'd talk about his family and especially his beloved dogs.

After the semester ended, I received a message from Jack's parents. Now, as a college instructor, you never want to hear from a parent. It's usually bad news. But in this case, Jack's parents said that Jack had given them permission to contact me and invite me out to lunch. They wanted to meet me.

I joined this couple for lunch, and as they shared about Jack, I couldn't believe my ears. The mother described how they feared they might lose Jack to alcohol and partying now that he was twenty-one. They worried about the friends he might spend time with. And then, Jack began talking about this Christian professor who didn't get drunk and who loved Jesus. The Holy Spirit began stirring in Jack's heart, and he returned to church and even began serving in the youth group.

As the mother shared this story, she said, "I just kept praying. I kept praying that God would send someone to turn him back!" All I heard was that word "turn" because I had prayed so fervently that God would "turn" Jack's eyes from worthless things. When I told the mother about my specific prayer from Psalm 119, she burst into tears. The father, too, looked overcome. He said, "If ever you think that what you are doing is not worth it, I want you to think of my son. We were so worried about Jack, and God sent you."

God sent me.

What if you are the answer to someone's prayer about a child or a friend? What if you entered your workplace as a royal priest sent to pronounce blessing and lead people to Jesus?

The final aspect of my royal priest identity that changed how I interact with others involves the priestly role of *explaining God's Word to people*. In fact, 1 Peter 2:9 brings the astonishing claim that we might all read and understand God's Word—not just the priests. Over the last few years, I've taken this priestly role more seriously; I actively try to weave God's Word into any conversation. It's part of my job description as a royal priest (just like the farmer who sows the Word).

Living as a sent person, I carry God's Word into the spaces I enter. I become like the person in Colossians 3:16 where Paul writes, "Let the word of Christ richly dwell within you, with all wisdom teaching and admonishing one another . . ." (NASB). Sent royal priests know that the Word of God is "God-breathed and is useful for teaching, rebuking, correcting and training in righteousness" (2 Tim. 3:16). They know that "the word of God is alive and active. Sharper than any double-edged sword, it penetrates even to dividing soul and spirit, joints and marrow; it judges the thoughts and attitudes of the heart" (Heb. 4:12). They know their own words don't carry the convicting power of God's Word. It is God's Word that changes people by the power of the Holy Spirit.

As I think about living my sent life as a royal priest, I remember that God's Word matters more than my argumentation. Charles Spurgeon tells us to "be walking Bibles."[7] He once preached how, "if we want revivals, we must revive our reverence for the Word of God. If we want conversions, we must put more of God's Word into our sermons—even if we paraphrase it into our own words, it must still be his Word upon which we place our reliance—for the only power which will bless men lies in that. It is God's Word that saves souls not our comment upon it, however correct that comment may be."[8] As a preacher, he finally concluded: "It is better to preach five words of God's word than five million words of man's wisdom. Men's words may seem to be the wiser and the more attractive, but there is no heavenly life in them."[9]

Sent royal priests offer the "heavenly life" from God's Word because they believe, as preacher and theologian Dr. Stephen Lawson stated in his exposition of Hebrews 4:12 on the living and active power of God's Word, that:

> The Bible claims to be "alive" (*zon*), meaning it is full of life—divine life, supernatural life, the very life of God Himself. Every other book is a dead book, devoid of life. But not the Bible. It alone is alive, always relevant, never stagnant. Martin Luther said, "The Bible is alive, it speaks to me; It has feet, it runs after me; it has hands, it lays hold on me." . . .
>
> When Scripture is preached, it is always energetic, always working, always executing God's sovereign purposes. God has said, "So shall My Word be which goes forth from my mouth; It shall not return to Me empty, without accomplishing what I desire, and without succeeding in the matter for which I sent it" (Isaiah 55:11). Wherever God's Word goes forth, it is always working to accomplish God's will. It never fails to succeed in the work for which it is intended. In other words, it is always capable to fulfill God's eternal purposes on the earth.[10]

I love Dr. Lawson's words because they remind me of the life, power, and purposes accomplished when I speak God's Word into a conversation. As I speak God's Word, I know that it's the most powerful tool available to me in my sent life. After all, as God Himself declares in Jeremiah 23:29: "Is not my word like fire . . . and like a hammer that breaks a rock in pieces?" Sent royal priests know the power of God's Word as they speak to others.

———————————※———————————

As you move into these four titles and job descriptions, you might find yourself growing in confidence and eagerness to live out these metaphors more and more. Barna's report on evangelism claims that, "Those who had at least one conversation about faith came away more confident and eager to talk with others. Nearly nine out of 10 say they are more confident in their own faith (86%) and seven out of 10 report being more eager to share their faith again (71%)."[11] How exciting! As you embrace the wonderful dimensions of these metaphors, finally remember their descriptions as hardworking, patient, confident, and authoritative. Wherever you go, God will develop these qualities in you as you trust Him to enter into the lives of the people around you.

YOUR SENT LIFE

Consider / Discuss

1. What images and feelings come to mind when you see yourself as "sent"?

2. What evidence do you find that God chose you for your exact location (home, neighborhood, workplace)?

3. Which biblical metaphor (farmer, fisherman, ambassador, or royal priest) most resonates with you and why?

4. Choose one of the metaphors above. How does this title and job description change how you behave in your home, neighborhood, and workplace?

Steps of Faith:

1. Map out your natural pathways. Where do you go? Where do you spend the most time during the day? Where do you find yourself on the weekends?

2. Would you add any new names to your list of five people?

3. Take some notes on each metaphor and your personal application of each title. How could you be more like the hardworking farmer, the patient fisherman, the confident ambassador, and the authoritative royal priest?

4. Begin collecting your favorite passages of Scripture. Try to use a few of these passages in a conversation this week. You might say, "This reminds me of something I just read in the Bible." Or try simply telling people that you are learning to memorize Scripture and wanted to share something you've memorized.

CHAPTER 4

Believing in Supernatural Power

But you will receive power when the Holy Spirit comes on
you; and you will be my witnesses in Jerusalem, and in all
Judea and Samaria, and to the ends of the earth.

—Acts 1:8

Jesus was eager for His disciples to wholeheartedly embrace the
new identity He had given them as *sent ones* and to embark
on the incredible adventure He gifted to them to reconcile others
to Himself. However, the very first charge He gave them wasn't to
launch out into evangelism.

He actually tells them to *wait*.

Doesn't that seem strange to you especially given how passion-
ately Jesus sought to send them out? What could possibly be so
important that Jesus' first move was to pump the brakes and bring
the mission of the church seemingly to a complete halt? For what
did He call them to wait? It wasn't for more training. It wasn't for
particular cultural or societal circumstances to develop. In fact, it
wasn't for a "what" that He called them to wait. It was for a "who."

He ordered them to wait for the Holy Spirit to come. But why?
It's because both the disciples and we today cannot do the work of

evangelism or live a sent life apart from the direction, wisdom, and power of the Holy Spirit. Even if we wholeheartedly embrace the three core principles of a sent life (see chapter 1), believe the gospel, and see the lostness of people apart from Christ, and even if we begin to live out the four biblical metaphors for evangelism we discussed in chapter 3, we will not bear fruit apart from Christ. We have learned the truth of Jesus' words in John 15:5: *Apart from me you can do nothing.*

We need the Holy Spirit to live a sent life. There's no other way to live as a sent person.

As the Scriptures proclaim, God didn't just send the Holy Spirit to Jesus' first disciples. God has sent the Holy Spirit to every believer. The Holy Spirit indwells every person who has received Christ into his or her life. So as we consider our identity as *sent ones*, we should be filled with excitement and expectation. God Himself living His life in and through us is primary to our identity as *sent ones*. The Holy Spirit is working through you to lead others to salvation.

However, many of us fail to see the Holy Spirit working through us to lead others to Jesus. Why is this the case? Shouldn't the Holy Spirit's work be just as unmistakable and present as Scripture's account of His work in creation, and the resurrection of Christ, and in the lives of His first disciples? Shouldn't we see the kind of response to the gospel as we see in Peter's and Paul's work throughout the book of Acts?

Yes!

Perhaps we have never been taught well about the person and ministry of the Holy Spirit. Or perhaps we have forgotten what we have been taught. Or perhaps we don't practically understand the role of the Holy Spirit in our lives and how to cooperate with

Him day by day, moment by moment, to live sent lives. I want to take a few minutes and share with you the role the Holy Spirit was designed to play in every believer's life as the foundation for our sent life.

In our ministry with Cru, we often refer to the "Spirit-filled life" as the foundational training in evangelism. In fact, Cru's founder, Bill Bright, defined success in evangelism as "sharing Christ in

> *The essence of the Christian life isn't what you do for God. The essence of the Christian life is what He does in and through you.*

the power of the Holy Spirit and leaving the results to God."[1] Once we understand the Spirit-filled life, we better understand how the Holy Spirit directs us to places and people who need to know Jesus—just as we see throughout the books of Acts. The Holy Spirit also gives us wisdom in evangelism and does the work of convicting the listener of their need for salvation (John 16:8).

I (Ashley) remember well my life and walk with Christ before understanding the role of the Holy Spirit. I was living how I think many Christians live. I was just trying to gut out the Christian life in my own strength. I was trying to pull myself up by my spiritual bootstraps. I really believed that God saved me and erased my sinful past, and that then it was on me to not mess it up again and go forward. I already knew the Christian life was really difficult as I tried to make good choices and live a godly life. But then I learned that the Christian life isn't just really difficult; it's actually impossible apart from the Holy Spirit working in our life.

The One who saved us also lives within us, and I no longer, you no longer, every believer across the globe no longer has to live the Christian life on his or her own. As we learned early on in our missionary training, the essence of the Christian life isn't what you do for God. The essence of the Christian life is what He does in and through you.

I began to understand this in my early twenties when I first noticed how remarkably the first disciples lived. In particular, the life of Paul especially captivated me. I wondered if his life was typical for believers or if it was the exception. Or perhaps God gifted him in really unique ways and he just was faithful to live out his giftings with extraordinary discipline and self-will. But that's not how Paul understood what was happening to him.

In Galatians 2:20 Paul says, "I have been crucified with Christ and I no longer live, but Christ lives in me. The life I now live in the body, I live by faith in the Son of God, who loved me and gave himself for me." Do you see what he is saying? He is saying, *Don't look to me. It's not me anymore. It's Christ living in me. I'm not impressing you. It's the Holy Spirit living His life out through my life that is impressing you.*

I began asking the Lord if Paul's crucified life was unique to him or available to all believers. I found my answer from a prayer Paul wrote in his letter to the Ephesians. He prays that your heart would be "enlightened in order that you may know the hope to which he has called you, the riches of his glorious inheritance in his holy people, and his incomparably great power for us who believe. That power is the same as the mighty strength he exerted when he raised Christ from the dead and seated him at his right hand in the heavenly realms" (Eph. 1:18–20).

Consider this great power available to us: it's the exact same power that raised Christ from the dead. That's not a little bit of power. That's *immeasurably great* power. And that exact same power right now resides in each of us. Scripture makes no bones about it. We are called to live a supernatural life. We get to live a supernatural life. We don't have capes; we don't fly. But we do become part of bringing dead people back to life in Christ as sent ones.

Something fundamentally changed when we became believers. In addition to forgiveness, redemption, and eternal life, God's power now fully indwells us. Paul prays later in Ephesians 3 "that out of his glorious riches he may strengthen you with *power through his Spirit* in your inner being" (v. 16). He goes on to pray, "Now to him who is able to do immeasurably more than all we ask or imagine, according *to his power that is at work within us*, to him be glory in the church and in Christ Jesus throughout all generations, for ever and ever! Amen" (vv. 20–21).

The Holy Spirit is so vital to our Christian lives, in fact, that Paul commands us to be filled with the Spirit. Paul instructs us in Ephesians 5:18: "Do not get drunk on wine, which leads to debauchery. Instead, be filled with the Spirit." The key word in this passage (besides "Spirit") is "filled."

But what does that word mean? There are at least two ways we can use the word "filled."

One way uses "filled" to communicate that we have received more of something. When we put more water in a glass, we say that the glass has been filled. So, we could understand "filled" in this passage to mean that we are commanded to get more of the Holy Spirit. But that's actually not what this verse says. Here's why. The Spirit is not a force or some inanimate object. The Spirit is much better. The Spirit is a person—a distinct member of the Trinity. And we get all of a person. We don't get the "arm" of God one day and then another part of God another day. No, we get all of God we are ever going to get when He indwells us—and that is all of Him. And so being filled with the Spirit is not getting more of the Spirit.

There's another way that we can use the word "filled." We use it when we say things like we are filled with rage or filled with joy. What do we mean when we say, "I'm filled with joy"? We mean that joy *has taken over and is controlling us.* That is how God is using "filled" in Ephesians 5. Being filled with the Spirit is not getting more of the Spirit. It is the Spirit getting more of me.

We allow the Holy Spirit to take over and control each of us. Furthermore, the Bible shows us that the Holy Spirit controls through two means—direction and empowerment. In short, living a Spirit-filled life is asking God to show me what to do and to give me the power to do it. Being filled by the Spirit means being directed and empowered by the Spirit. So, as the Spirit gets more of me, He controls me by giving me the power to do what He wants and directs me to do. Whenever that happens, God is living His supernatural life in and through me. That's the way God designed the Christian life to function.

Surrendering to the Holy Spirit's direction and empowerment is clearly God's plan for our life. As you study the Greek tense of the verb for "filled," you discover that Paul's command reads like this: "keep on being filled with the Spirit." It's not a one-time experience or command. Paul is commanding us to moment by moment keep on being controlled and empowered (i.e., filled) by the Holy Spirit.

To live a Spirit-filled life, we might ask: "What does Jesus want to do in and through my life?" It's closer to what Paul is commanding. However, that question could lead us to think that most of the time we just do what we want to do except for those special moments or seasons when we give control to Jesus (e.g., when taking a step of faith to do something for God like serving in church or going on a mission trip).

Instead, consider this question to lead a Spirit-filled life:

"What does Jesus want to do in and through my life that I am not allowing Him to?" Here's why. The moment-by-moment norm for our new life in Christ is that every moment Jesus is living His life in and through us. That should be the expectation. That shouldn't be a special case. That shouldn't just be a "great day." It should be every day. This is what God has gifted every believer for every moment for the rest of their lives. As Jesus lives His life in and through us by His Spirit, He will do great and wondrous things. That is, unless we keep Him from doing so.

If this is supposed to be God's plan, God's expectation, God's desire for our life, why is this not happening every moment of our life? Well, it's because we get in the way of God doing so. We cause it to not happen. We can take control back from God and keep the Spirit from operating at times in our life. There are two main ways this happens: sin and self-effort.

Galatians 5:17 says the first way that we keep the Spirit from empowering and directing our life is our sinful nature or what the Bible calls our "flesh." Paul writes, "For the flesh desires what is contrary to the Spirit, and the Spirit what is contrary to the flesh. They are in conflict with each other, so that you are not to do whatever you want."

In other words, we have still have our old sin nature (our flesh). One day, praise God, that will be removed. Right now the power of sin has been broken and the penalty of sin has been broken, but the presence of sin still remains. As believers, a battle rages for who will control our lives at any moment. Either the Holy Spirit will control us, or our old sin nature will control us. So what keeps the Spirit from working? It's sin.

But there's a second way we keep the Spirit from empowering and directing us. Galatians 3:3 asks, "Are you so foolish? After beginning by means of the Spirit, are you now trying to finish by means of the flesh?" Self-effort (or trying to work "by means of the flesh") keeps the Spirit from filling us. As we mature in Christ, we are tempted to believe the lie that we can increasingly live the Christian life on our own. We are meant to live supernatural lives. But why don't our lives look supernatural at times? Could it be that we are attempting to live a supernatural life by very ordinary means? God calls us to trust Him, and then He wants us to depend on Him, yield to Him, and see Him work in supernatural, wonderful ways. That's why the disciples had to wait before they launched out into their sent lives. *They needed the Holy Spirit first.* And we must wait, too. We often rush and fail to pray for direction or power.

The Spirit-filled life calls us to move from independence to dependence on God and from taking control to yielding control of our lives to God. Jesus said, "Remain in me, as I also remain in you. No branch can bear fruit by itself; it must remain in the vine. Neither can you bear fruit unless you remain in me. I am the vine; you are the branches. If you remain in me and I in you, you will bear much fruit; apart from me you can do nothing" (John 15:4–5). The Spirit's role is to empower and to direct. Thus, our role is to remain in Christ by depending on and yielding to God. If God, the all-powerful One, is empowering us, the best thing we can do is to depend on Him and His power. If God, the sovereign, all-knowing One, is directing us, the best thing we can do is to yield to that direction.

So how do we live the Spirit-filled life? In particular, if we have taken back control of our life from God, how do we return to being filled by the Holy Spirt? We acknowledge to God that we have taken control from Him and want Him to once again control (empower and direct) our lives. The first step is to confess any unconfessed sin to God. If there's something blocking the Spirit from working, we simply need to confess it to God.

The second step is to surrender every area of our lives to Christ. If there is a part of our life that we have taken control of, we just need to hand it back over to God with a heart attitude of dependence and yielding to Him. And then by faith we need to trust the Holy Spirit to fill us in response to God's command and promise. First John 5:14–15 promises, "This is the confidence we have in approaching God: that if we ask anything according to his will, he hears us. And if we know that he hears us—whatever we ask—we know that we have what we asked of him."

Once we have asked the Holy Spirit to fill us again, we then move forward by faith and live our lives yielded to and in dependence on the Spirit. Whenever we find that we have taken back control, we simply return to confessing sin, surrendering, and asking for the Spirit to fill us again.

In fact, I want to give you a few moments right now to meet with God and ask the Holy Spirit to fill you again if needed. If you'd like, you can use the following prayer found in Cru's *Satisfied* booklet.

> Dear Father, I need You. I acknowledge that I have sinned against You by directing my own life. I thank You that You have forgiven my sins through Christ's death on the cross for me. I now invite Christ to again take His place on the throne of my life. Fill me with the Holy Spirit as you commanded me to be filled, and as You promised in Your Word that You would do if I asked in faith. I pray this in the name of Jesus. I now thank you for filling me with the Holy Spirit and directing my life.[2]

If needed, I hope you just took a few minutes and asked the Spirit to fill you again. We'd love for everyone reading to leave this chapter filled with God's Spirit as the starting place for their sent life. What we offer a spiritually dying world is Christ living His life through us by His Spirit. This is who we get to take with us into the lives of those God has placed around us. And this is who they need. They don't need to see us striving to live the Christian life on our own. They need to see Jesus living His life through us.

———————✳———————

I (Heather) take great comfort in the biblical roles the Holy Spirit assumes in Scripture that we know work in our own lives as well. These roles provide the foundation of living a supernatural life.

The Holy Spirit gives courage and boldness to act and speak (Acts 4:31) when we're afraid.

He compels us to action (Acts 20:22)—to go to certain places and speak to various people.

He leads us where He wants us to go (Matt. 4:1; Rom. 8:14; Acts 16:6–7).

He speaks through us and give us words to say (Matt. 10:20; Mark 13:11; Luke 12:12).

He gives us wisdom and understanding (Col. 1:9).

It is the Holy Spirit who convicts people of their sin (John 16:8) and produces new life in them as they come to Jesus (John 6:63; Titus 3:5). As I understand more and more why I need the Holy Spirit to live a sent life, I become so excited to imagine what my life will look like as I yield more and more control to Him.

I also become excited when I remember this: As the disciples waited at the beginning of the book of Acts, they model a key practice that undergirds a sent life. While the disciples waited, they weren't just staring at the wall. They were doing perhaps the greatest work they could do at that moment:

They were praying.

————————— ✳ —————————

What do people living a sent life pray for? The Holy Spirit intercedes for us as noted in Romans 8:26 and guides us as we pray for others. I began to look for biblical models of prayer for people who don't yet know Jesus or who are just starting out on their spiritual journey.

Consider the five people on your list that you've already started to pray for. Consider again the family members, neighbors, and those in our natural pathways of work, errands, the gym, or any other location in which we find ourselves. Before jumping right into evangelism apart from the wisdom, direction, and empowerment of the Holy Spirit, we invite you first to pray for these people by name every day and wait to see how the Lord is working. But what do we pray? Throughout the Bible, we ask God for the same things we see the biblical writers praying about as led by the Holy Spirit. I have found these verses particularly inspiring and instructive:

SEVEN WAYS TO PRAY FOR
THOSE WHO DON'T YET KNOW JESUS

1. Ask God to send a "Spirit of wisdom and revelation" to that person.

Paul writes this in Ephesians 1:17–19:

> I keep asking that the God of our Lord Jesus Christ, the glorious Father, may give you the Spirit of wisdom and revelation, so that you may know him better. I pray that the eyes of your heart may be enlightened in order that you may know the hope to which he has called you, the riches of his glorious inheritance in his holy people, and his incomparably great power for us who believe.

Many times in the process of praying for people on my list, one of them approached me to talk about how they have sensed God stirring in them or drawing them to spiritual things. Living a sent life means we understand the work of the Holy Spirit to draw others to Jesus; we simply participate in what *God is already doing*. I have prayed this passage in Ephesians for a neighbor who suddenly began wondering about Jesus and His claim to be the "way and the truth and the life" (John 14:6).

As we prayed for neighbors to experience a drawing of them toward Jesus, I'll never forget the day my husband invited some professors to study the book of John with us. I was nervous because I didn't sense God at work in their lives, but Ashley wanted to step out in faith since we had been praying for months for these friends. When we invited them, the professor I thought had no interest in

Jesus exclaimed, "I have been waiting for an invitation like this!"

Right now, who has the Lord laid on your heart to pray this prayer from Ephesians? Take a moment and ask God to send the Spirit of wisdom and revelation so that person will understand who Jesus is. Pray that the "eyes of [his or her] heart may be enlightened." You might not see the results of your prayers immediately. A particular couple we'd been praying about for over twenty-five years called one Saturday morning to tell Ashley and me that they began to attend a church and are seeking the Lord. I wrote in my journal a prayer of thanks that God had indeed answered that prayer. My mentor prayed for twenty years for her sister to come to know Jesus, and she finally did. Asking God for that spirit of revelation might be a prayer you persevere in for years.

2. Ask God to "turn [their] eyes away from worthless things" and that they "come to their senses."

In Psalm 119:37, the priest asks the Lord this: "Turn my eyes away from worthless things . . ." I pray this for myself, but I also pray this for others in my life who begin to walk down the dark and slippery paths of sin. I pray Psalm 119:37 for people on my list who seek spiritual truth apart from Jesus. I have several friends, for example, who see spirit-channelers, psychics, and mediums. I have friends who spend a fortune on New Age practices for healing. One night, after over a year of talking with a friend about Jesus, I felt especially frustrated with her attempts to find guidance and healing using techniques I felt were either scams or demonic. So I prayed in my living room a desperate prayer that God would expose the lies of the enemy and turn her eyes from worthless things. I prayed from 2 Timothy 2:25–26 where Paul writes this:

Opponents must be gently instructed, in the hope that God will grant them repentance leading them to a knowledge of the truth, and that they will come to their senses and escape from the trap of the devil, who has taken them captive to do his will.

I notice, here, how Paul advises *gentle instruction* as we engage others with the gospel. I also notice how it is God who grants repentance that leads to truth. But mostly, I notice why we need this work of God: so that others come to their right mind and escape the trap of the devil. Then I shudder at this final truth of how the devil takes others captive to do his will. What a mighty and vital prayer to ask that God release our friends and family from the trap of the devil!

As I prayed both Psalm 119 and 2 Timothy over my friend, an hour later, my phone rang. My friend said, "You know, I've been on this [New Age] path for twelve years. I have no peace and no healing. Where is this path taking me?" Soon after, she prayed to receive Christ.

Who in your life might you pray for now who needs to turn their eyes from worthless things? Who do you feel has been ensnared by the devil? Begin praying right now that God would do the great work described in 2 Timothy 2.

3. Ask God to send others to help.

In Matthew 9:38, Jesus says to "ask the Lord of the harvest . . . to send out workers into his harvest field." I love this prayer as I think about our children going off to college. I pray that God brings people into their lives who know Jesus and who might help our daughters continue to grow in the Lord. I like to remember that

God sent the disciples two by two (Mark 6:7). I often feel alone in my sent life, especially if I'm praying for friends who don't know other Christians.

Recently, I felt overwhelmed in my conversations with a certain colleague. Her questions often stumped me, and she toggled back and forth between belief in Jesus and then a return to a universalist position that all paths lead to God. She also paid money to contact the dead for wisdom and advice for her future. I prayed one morning that God would bring someone else to help me. I said, "God, please send someone else like me who will talk to her about You." During a phone call a few days later, my friend began talking about a new Christian friend that she'd reunited with who talked about Jesus and invited her to church. She said, "She's exactly like you!"

I've also prayed for people on my list that God would cause Christian neighbors, coworkers, and new friends to enter into their lives. When I hear about these Christians, I write down in my prayer journal that God has answered my prayer to send others to help.

4. Ask God for an open door for the gospel.
In Colossians 4:2–4, we read some of the most encouraging words for our sent life. Paul writes this:

> Devote yourselves to prayer, being watchful and thankful. And pray for us, too, that God may open a door for our message, so that we may proclaim the mystery of Christ, for which I am in chains. Pray that I may proclaim it clearly, as I should.

I love this call to devote ourselves to prayer. And why would Paul instruct us to stay *watchful*? It's a wonderful posture of anticipation of where God is working and how He is moving in the lives of others. Paul asks that God would "open a door" for the message of God, and he further requests that God give him clarity in his presentation. As I interact with my community, I pray this prayer most of all.

A few semesters ago, I began to pray this prayer for my students. I sensed so much anxiety, confusion, and even despair in many of my students. I prayed that God would open a door so I may appropriately talk about Jesus. Maybe someone would ask me about God during office hours. Maybe a student would ask me about my life in a way that would invite me to discuss Jesus. I knew God had answered the prayer in the past when it was Roco who called out in front of the whole class one day, "Dr. H, can you tell us why you chose Christianity as opposed to any other religion? We really want to know!" I told the class I would be happy to share my story in my office hours or if they wanted to go out for coffee so I could use my class time for writing instruction, but Kathryn raised her hand and said, "Can you at least tell us where to start reading in the Bible if we were interested?"

Another semester, Joe stopped the whole class and said, "You've got to tell us the secret of why you're so happy all the time" and that led to an honest conversation about my faith in Christ. In fact, the most common open door for the gospel I have with younger people involves me telling them my "secret" for joyful living.

At a coffee shop one afternoon, my student Muriel said, "Okay, so why are you so happy? Do you take a certain drug?"

I laughed and said, "I believe you are sensing the presence of the Living God, Jesus Christ, within me. He is the source of my joy and peace."

With wide eyes, Muriel said, "Well, I'm really into yoga. I believe that anything we do can lead us to spiritual truth. So I do not know about Jesus."

I said, "Would you like to read a book about Jesus? It's called *The Reason for God*, by Tim Keller." In the past, I had given students *More Than a Carpenter* by Josh McDowell, but as the years went by, I liked using *Mere Christianity* by C. S. Lewis and *Jesus Among Other Gods* by Ravi Zacharias as well as *The Reason for God* by Tim Keller with seeking students. This student read Keller's book and returned the next week to say, "I cannot deny that Jesus is the Lord. I've prayed to invite Jesus into my life. But can you help me? I need a Bible!" Months later, I attended her baptism.

As I prayed the Colossians prayer on the last day of my most recent semester with my class of despairing students, I couldn't believe what happened next. First, my student Frank asked—completely out of the blue—if I knew whether the God of the Old Testament was the same God described in the New Testament. That opened the door. Then, two of my most brilliant students approached my podium. They wanted to know about my philosophy of living. David said he was so curious about faith, and Rebecca leaned over and said, "If you know the truth, you have to tell us. What is the truth?"

I said, "It's Jesus, if you want to know the truth. Everything we're searching for in life is about Him."

David said, "Yeah, my friend is always trying to get me to read the Bible with him."

"You should!" I said. "I'd start with the book of John."

"Okay, I will."

I smiled and packed up my teaching bag of notes, chalk, and lists of vivid verbs. God did not fail to open the door, even though it took an entire semester.

5. Ask God to give you boldness to overcome your fear.

I recently noticed something amazing in the book of Ephesians. One day, when I was reading Ephesians 6, I took note that Paul asks for personal prayer. He only does so a few times in the New Testament, so I paid attention. What would Paul ask for? A wife? To be released from prison? For more money? I thought of all the things a person might ask for when they request personal prayer.

But no. Paul asks for something astonishing. This is his request in Ephesians 6:19–20:

> Pray also for me, that whenever I speak, words may be given me so that I will fearlessly make known the mystery of the gospel, for which I am an ambassador in chains. Pray that I may declare it fearlessly, as I should.

Oh, how I love this prayer! I love that, like me, Paul needed *courage*. Notice how he repeats that word "fearlessly" twice. He prays that he will "fearlessly" declare, and I pray the same courage for myself. I find it fascinating and deeply inspiring that Paul wanted nothing more than words to make Jesus known. In your own list of people for whom you pray, which person requires the most courage and why? For me, I pray for courage when speaking to people who sometimes intimidate me like supervisors, highly intelligent people, or those known for loving arguments.

Since Paul admits his need for fearless proclamation, I sometimes tell people I'm nervous or scared to begin conversations with them, especially if I'm talking to someone who has been hurt by the church or by other Christians. I'm afraid of offending them, saying the wrong thing, or causing further damage by the way I speak. So sometimes I simply say that to them. I say, "As we talk about Jesus, I just want you to know I've prayed for courage and clarity.

I'm afraid of not communicating God's love clearly to you! I'm also afraid that you will categorize me as hateful or mindless." This statement disarms others and lets you move into gospel conversations with honesty and love.

Jesus, I want to live a sent life. I am available for You to use me when, where, and how You wish.

6. Pray the message of Christ spreads quickly.

I pray the same prayer Paul requests of us in 2 Thessalonians 3:1. He writes, "As for other matters, brothers and sisters, pray for us that the message of the Lord may spread rapidly and be honored, just as it was with you."

I'm an impatient person. I don't want to wait long for others to receive Christ. That's why I love praying that the message *spreads rapidly*. Right now, as you consider your family, community, and workplace, ask God to allow the gospel to spread rapidly throughout that location. As I think about historic revivals on college campuses or in small towns, I find myself overcome with excitement that I might, in my lifetime, see a rapid spread of the gospel.

7. Ask God to continue to instruct you in *when, where, how,* and *to whom* He would like you to communicate the gospel.

Lately, I've been meditating on Psalm 32:8 where David writes this about God: "I will instruct you and teach you in the way you should go; I will counsel you with my loving eye on you." If reading this book overwhelms you because you simply have no idea how to engage others in gospel conversations, pray for God to continue to instruct you and lead you. Pray for His counsel to fill your mind as you read on into the next section that trains you for a lifetime of Spirit-filled adventure.

You might pray a prayer like this:

> *Jesus, I want to live a sent life. I am available for You to use me when, where, and how You wish. Teach me how to live a life that You commanded and empower me to live. Thank You for the Holy Spirit who is doing this work in me now.*

SEVEN WAYS TO PRAY

1. Ask God to send a "Spirit of wisdom and revelation" to that person.—Ephesians 1:17–19
2. Ask God to "turn [their] eyes from worthless things" and that they "come to their senses."—Psalm 119:37
3. Ask God to send others to help.—Matthew 9:38
4. Ask God for an open door for the gospel.—Colossians 4:2–4

5. Ask God to give you boldness to overcome your fear.
   —Ephesians 6:19–20

6. Pray the message of Christ spreads quickly.—2 Thessalonians 3:1

7. Ask God to continue to instruct you in *when, where, how,* and *to whom* He would like you to communicate the gospel.—Psalm 32:8

Because you are now filled with the Holy Spirit, you'll feel fresh power, wisdom, and expectancy as you pray, and you'll find yourself inspired to persevere in prayer for the people in your life who don't yet know Jesus.

YOUR SENT LIFE

Consider / Discuss

1. Explain in your own words what it means to "be filled with the Holy Spirit."

2. When was the last time you felt supernaturally directed by the Holy Spirit?

3. Why do you think you need the Holy Spirit to live a sent life? What does the Holy Spirit do?

4. In the Seven Ways to Pray, which prayer did God answer in your own life to bring you to Jesus?

Steps of Faith:

1. Take a moment and ask God to fill you with the Holy Spirit by confessing all known sin and expressing your desire to allow the Holy Spirit to control and direct all areas of your life.

2. Take your list of five people and begin praying for each according to the Seven Ways to Pray.

3. How is the Holy Spirit prompting you in regard to the people in your life? Take a few quiet moments and see if the Holy Spirit impresses on your heart a way to pray, a way to reach out, or a place to go.

4. If you wish, design your own prayer journal where you now leave room to record where you see God at work to answer your prayers for the people on your list.

PART 2

LIVING LIKE A SENT PERSON

CHAPTER 5

The World We're Sent Into

But the LORD said to me, "Do not say, 'I am too young.' You must go to everyone I send you to and say whatever I command you. Do not be afraid of them, for I am with you and will rescue you," declares the LORD.

—Jeremiah 1:7–8

As Christians, we have been given a new identity as *sent ones* and have been sent by God into the world to bring the hope and love of Christ. But what world has God sent us into?

At first glance, the picture doesn't look too rosy—at least in North America and Western Europe currently. At the time of this writing, the 2019 Pew Research survey indicated the decline of Christianity at a "rapid pace." The report shares that "65% of American adults describe themselves as Christians when asked about their religion, down 12 percentage points over the past decade. Meanwhile, the religiously unaffiliated share of the population, consisting of people who describe their religious identity as atheist, agnostic or 'nothing in particular,' now stands at 26%, up from 17% in 2009."[1]

While these numbers seem discouraging, other surveys tell us that "religion is on the wane in western Europe and North America and it's growing everywhere else."[2] Pew also reported that "Christianity has grown enormously in sub-Saharan Africa and the Asia-Pacific region, where there were relatively few Christians at the beginning of the 20th century. The share of the population that is Christian in sub-Saharan Africa climbed from 9% in 1910 to 63% in 2010, while in the Asia-Pacific region it rose from 3% to 7%. Christianity today—unlike a century ago—is truly a global faith."[3]

Those numbers are super encouraging. We ought to celebrate, thank the Lord, and find ways to encourage our brothers and sisters in Christ in those areas of the world to keep going. But the story of God's work in sub-Saharan Africa and the Asia-Pacific region also offers us something else. Don't miss it! *It shows us the power of a sent life.* God raised up believers—both from within those regions and from outside those regions—and sent them to those who didn't yet know Him. They embraced their identity as *sent ones* and the rest is history.

However, you might find yourself in a community—or part of the world—where the state of Christianity or spiritual interest discourages you or overwhelms you. You might not know where to begin. You might feel like God can't possibly be at work around you. We invite you to remember that over one hundred years ago, the spiritual need of sub-Saharan Africa and the Asia-Pacific region was so great, it mobilized Christians to embrace their identity as *sent ones.* Likewise, we invite you to embrace your identity as a *sent one.* For such a time as this, the time is right to begin living a sent life.

Perhaps at the time you are reading this book, the state of Christianity has become more dire. Or perhaps we're seeing revival. Either way, we don't embrace a sent life in spite of the current climate for the gospel. We embrace a sent life *because* of the current climate for the gospel.

If we embrace our sent life because of the current climate of the gospel—not in spite of that climate—then we need to think wisely and thoughtfully about the way we do so. At the time of this writing, many of the people we begin to equip and coach to live as *sent ones* arrive with an understanding of evangelism that *only* practically involves sharing a plan of salvation (for example, using tools like *Romans Road to Salvation*, the Navigators' *Bridge Illustration*, or Cru's *Knowing God Personally*). However, the people they want to talk to about Jesus may not even be sure that God exists. Or they may not believe in heaven. Or they haven't ever considered the eternity of the soul. The people they want to share Jesus with may not know or understand biblical language and stories. Additionally, they may not have a church background. It could even be that they don't have a positive view of the church or Christianity.

In other words, the sent ones we are equipping and coaching are experiencing a disconnect between the evangelism approaches and tools they know of, or possibly have heard of, and the world they live in. The idea of sharing a plan of salvation as the only evangelism activity seems outdated and out of place for sharing Christ with others in the world we live in today. In response, some have stopped using tools that clearly communicate the gospel. Others push through their hesitations and continue to only share a plan for salvation in every situation.

We'd like to suggest a third perspective: simply discover where a person is spiritually. Do they think about spiritual things? Do they believe in God? Do they believe in an afterlife? What have they heard about Jesus? What does the word "sin" mean to them? Have they heard the word "salvation" before?

Our good friend and mentor, Randy Newman—yes, the same Randy Newman I (Ashley) wrote of in chapter 2—provides a useful way to think of this process of engaging others in spiritual conversations no matter where they fall in the spectrum of readiness to hear about Jesus.

Several years ago, Randy created a way to represent people's interest in Christ—or lack thereof—prior to placing their faith in Christ. Imagine a line with the letters A to Z distributed above it. Each letter represents a different point on this line. Letter A represents a person who would be the farthest away you could imagine from receiving Christ—perhaps a hardened atheist or someone who does not believe in any kind of spiritual reality. Letter Z, on the other end of the spectrum, represents one who is very interested in Christ and will likely receive Him into his or her life very soon. They understand they need forgiveness of sin and feel separated from God. They want to know Him and feel a sense of being drawn to Him. Letter T represents "people who already believe in God, think the Bible is probably worth listening to, and are already convinced they need forgiveness for some things they've done."[4]

Many of today's evangelism tools that clearly communicate the gospel were created in the middle of the twentieth century (by the way, that may be why some readers haven't heard of them). This was a time and world very different from the world we live in today in the United States. It was a time and world in which many non-Christians likely fell somewhere between T and Z on Randy's scale. They knew spiritual words like sin and salvation. They knew popular Bible stories. They most likely went to church with their family and other families in their neighborhood.

In other words, these evangelism tools were created at a time in history when many non-Christians were open and interested in learning about Jesus. However, many of the people who now cross our paths, and who don't know Jesus, more likely fall somewhere much closer to A–S (atheism or possible agnosticism). The problem isn't that tools designed to clearly communicate the gospel are outdated or out of place. They are neither. They depend on God's authoritative and powerful Word, and they are wonderfully effective for reaching those who fall somewhere between T and Z. A concise, clear, full explanation of the gospel and an invitation to respond to Jesus is exactly what those at these points in their spiritual journey want and need.

Instead, the challenge—and opportunity—is to also learn of and effectively use the tools and strategies most suited for our friends, family members, neighbors, and coworkers wherever they are in their spiritual journey. We

> *The journey doesn't always move in a straight line or at an equal pace—that's okay. Sometimes people take steps back before moving forward.*

need to grow our evangelism toolbox so that we have the right tools at the right time. These tools and strategies comprise the following chapters that both shape your own awareness of those around you and help you enter into their lives with good questions and your own stories of gospel transformation.

Additionally, the work of evangelism has shifted from singular gospel conversations to ongoing spiritual conversations that help others move one step at a time closer to responding to the gospel and receiving Christ into their life. To use the terminology of Randy's spiritual interest scale, we want to help others move from A to Z. In other words, those around us are now more likely to progressively journey to faith in Christ than they are to hear the gospel one time and place their faith in Christ. As *sent ones*, God calls us to enter into their lives and help them take the next steps in their spiritual journey toward Christ.

Author Doug Pollock calls this activity the creation of "God Space"—"low-risk, high-grace places for people to pursue their need to have spiritual conversations."[5] As Doug explains in his book *God Space*, God has given every person a real awareness of their need for Him. And we believe this as one of our core principles —that God is at work to draw people to Himself. Consequently, those around us are far more likely than we believe to explore their need for God if we will choose to take the initiative and create the kind of spaces where they feel safe to do so.

To see this happen, consider this outline of the steps Heather and I have learned to take to help others pursue ongoing spiritual conversations:

1. Move toward people through prayer (like the Seven Ways to Pray), gathering them together and caring for them (which we explore in chapter 7), and then take the initiative to begin a spiritual conversation.
2. Find out where a person is spiritually and what they need next to move forward in their spiritual journey toward Christ. And then consider what next conversation or tool would best meet that need (chapters 8 and 9).
3. Have the next conversation ending with the goal and desire of having the next and future conversations. You might say, "I hope we can talk more! What if we had coffee sometime next week? I'd love to hear about your spiritual journey and what you think about what we've been talking about."

And here are some helpful hints:

1. The journey doesn't always move in a straight line or at an equal pace—that's okay. Sometimes people take steps back before moving forward. Sometimes they leap several steps forward in a single conversation.
2. Be bold, take the initiative, but don't be disrespectful. If a person isn't interested in talking about God, you don't want to force the conversation.
3. You can always, and will need to, pray!
4. People are often more spiritually sensitive during times of disruption or hard times in their life. As you move into people's lives when they are hurting through illness or suffering of any kind, you can become an agent of blessing as you care for them and wait for opportunities to pray and talk about your hope in Christ through suffering.
5. If someone isn't all that interested in talking about spiritual things, keep talking about what God is doing in your own life, pray, and watch for their interest to return or surface.
6. You don't have to wait for a person to show complete spiritual interest to walk through the gospel with them. It can be really helpful early on for them to know and understand exactly what you believe about knowing God personally. Plus, God may want to move in their heart to respond. If God is leading you to do so, follow Him.

In the following four chapters, we will share many of the tools and strategies we have found most helpful in pursuing ongoing spiritual conversations with our friends, family members, neighbors, and coworkers no matter what kind of spiritual interest they

Many indicators show us people have lost interest in spiritual conversations, and the culture continues to lose an understanding of biblical language. But we are uniquely positioned to enter the lives of those we know, discover how God is at work, and begin having spiritual conversations.

demonstrate. In chapter 10, we will explain when and how we transition to sharing a concise, clear, full explanation of the gospel and invite someone to respond to Jesus.

But before we move on, I wanted to share one final thought that we hope will help you as much as it is helping us. Several weeks ago, Heather and I were walking through our neighborhood one evening as we talked about this chapter. This is not an easy chapter to write. The surveys we shared at the beginning of the chapter are truly useful and provide great perspective, but they always leave us feeling discouraged. In fact, Heather thought of many other indicators that show us people have lost interest in spiritual conversations, and the culture continues to lose an understanding of biblical language.

But we wondered if these surveys and trends we read truly reflect the hearts of the neighbors on our street, our coworkers, and the people we intersect in our community. Should we disengage from evangelism simply because it seems that people are less and less interested in God? We realized this: surveys cannot tell us everything we need to know about the specific people and places that comprise our unique lives.

And that is the point, isn't it? We don't know the details of the people in your neighborhood or workplace. We don't know your friends, family members, coworkers, and neighbors. But as we walked through our neighborhood one night several weeks ago, God reminded us we have the great opportunity to know the details of the people in our workplaces and community and who live on our streets—the very ones He has sent us to. We are uniquely positioned to enter their lives, discover how God is at work, and begin having spiritual conversations.

Likewise, you can too. All it takes is the commitment to see the people around you and discover some things about their lives.

We don't all have to become experts on the state of evangelism for the whole world. We just need to become experts on those God has sovereignly placed us next to—the exact world God has sent (and/or will send) each of us into. What an exciting adventure of discovery God gives each of us as we move toward those God has sent us to, learn about them and their world, and create the space to join them on their spiritual journey toward Christ.

YOUR SENT LIFE

Consider / Discuss

1. Describe the "spiritual climate" of your neighborhood, workplace, and larger community. Are people interested in going to church? Do they listen to worship music? Do they talk about spiritual things? Would they have a Bible in their home? Would they have been raised in a spiritual tradition?

2. Do you agree we're seeing a decline of Christianity at a "rapid pace" in our culture? What do you think accounts for this?

3. What do you think you need to pray for most of all for your community? What are the unique needs you see?

4. What do you think is the primary obstacle keeping people around you from coming to Jesus?

Steps of Faith:

1. Consider the five people on your list. If you were to place them on a spectrum of spiritual interest, where would you place them?

2. What is the next step you might take with one of the five people on your list to discover their spiritual interest? Write down your intention to have a conversation, invite a person to a Christian event, or do something else the Lord prompts you.

3. Take some time to pray for your neighborhood, workplace, and larger community.

4. Where do you see people suffering around you? Ask the Lord and take some time to consider how you might bless a hurting person and gauge their spiritual sensitivity.

CHAPTER 6

What Do You See?

Look, I tell you, lift up your eyes,
and see that the fields are white for harvest.
—Jesus in John 4:35 ESV

Several years ago I (Ashley) began noticing our eighty-five-year-old neighbor "Bill" and his faithful dog "Scout" walking by our house every morning at the same time. I noticed this because curiously I just so happened to regularly be outside at the exact same time the pair walked by. At first, I didn't think much about it. It was just a man and his dog walking by our house. Many other dogs and their owners have walked by our home over the years. Bill and I would both wave and say, "Good morning," but that was it. I'd head back into the house or go back to what I was doing while Bill and Scout continued on their daily walk.

It wasn't long, however, before God began calling me to reach out to Bill. Because of the uncanny near-daily frequency of our seeing each other, I easily realized that God had sovereignly placed Bill in my life for a purpose and that God was sending me to him.

But I fought God every step of the way. I suspected that Bill was twice my age. I couldn't imagine that we'd have much in common or that he would be all that interested in hearing what a guy half his age thought. And, to be honest, I assumed that given his age, his beliefs—whatever they might be—were unlikely to change.

I kept waving and calling out my "Hello!" and God kept prompting me to do something—anything—more. Finally, I relented and cooperated with God.

I took a step of faith.

As Bill and Scout walked by one day, I joked, "You know, if we keep saying 'Good morning' to each other, we should probably at least know each other's name." Bill laughed. We exchanged names and a few basic details. And then Bill and Scout continued their walk.

Instantly, God's Spirit convicted me that I could have engaged Bill much more than I did, and I felt prompted to invite him to coffee. I pledged that I would do so the very next time I saw Bill (knowing full well that I would be off the hook until at least the next day). Bill and Scout had a very regular walking time and path. You could set your watch by it. But that is not what happened next. For the first time—and only time—Bill and Scout turned around and started walking *back up my street.*

It was go-time. I knew I had to follow through with what I promised God. So as Bill walked by I yelled (he was on the other side of the street), "Hey Bill, would you ever like to get a cup of coffee?" He walked across the street and said, "I'd love to." But I didn't have to hear his words to know how much the invitation meant to him. His face told me everything I needed to know. You won't believe what happened next, which I'll share shortly.

Some of you are wondering what took me so long. Others are wondering if they would have ever reached out. Why? Why do some of us instantly jump in while others of us hesitate? There are several reasons why a lot of us hesitate, many of which we are seeking to address in this book. I want to share one of them here:

We don't see others the same way Jesus does.

In John 4, Jesus encounters a Samaritan woman and begins one of the most well-known gospel conversations of all time. As their conversation ends, Jesus' disciples return from buying food in a nearby city. They are amazed that Jesus was talking with the woman. They then encourage Him to eat and are perplexed when He says in verse 32, "I have food to eat that you know nothing about," because He doesn't have any physical food to eat. He explains, "My food . . . is to do the will of him who sent me and to finish his work" (v. 34). In other words, joining God, the Father, in the work of reconciling people back to Him was the "spiritual food" that deeply satisfied and nourished Jesus.

Then He gives them a remarkable invitation and command that will help them enjoy the same "spiritual food" He enjoys. He tells them in verse 35, "Look, I tell you, lift up your eyes, and see that the fields are white for harvest" (ESV). As they do, they see the Samaritan woman and many from her city walking toward them. The Samaritans ask Jesus to stay. He and His disciples stay for two days. And many of those who walked toward them plus many more believe in Jesus. I can't imagine that the disciples missed the point He was making.

He was training His disciples—and us—*to look up* and see those around them the same way He sees them. He sees them as men and women of infinite value, created by God to know Him, and more likely to respond to Jesus than we typically believe. As said earlier, this comes naturally for some of us. For the rest of us, how do we develop this desire and ability to see others the way Jesus does? It could be as simple as learning a new habit that will mark your life as a *sent one*.

*The "What Do You See?" campaign encourages us to daily **look up** from our distracted and isolated day to see who might be in our path at an exact moment. It totally works!*

In this chapter, we want to share a fun, engaging, and simple activity for developing this new habit of noticing and seeing others the way Jesus does. And then I'll tell you the rest of Bill's story.

We call this activity the "What Do You See?" campaign. We created it soon after launching our ministry to graduate students at Penn State University. The students we worked with loved Jesus and were open to living as *sent ones* who talked with those around them about Christ. However, they struggled to do so. They didn't easily notice those around them and see them the way Jesus does. We created the "What Do You See?" campaign to encourage our students to daily *look up* from their distracted and isolated workday to see who might be in their path at that exact moment. It totally worked!

They began noticing others more than they had before and seeing them as ones who needed to know Jesus. And they found great joy in engaging friends, family members, coworkers, and complete strangers in loving conversations. We have also used the campaign with participants in an evangelism class we teach at our church. It's had the same powerful impact for them as well.

The campaign involves sending the following short, four-word text: "What do you see?" When the campaign participants receive the randomized text (that comes once each day at various times), they simply *look up and see* who is in front of them or nearby them. And then they quietly pray and ask God to help them see that person the same way He does.

Perhaps they see the same person they see every week at the grocery store but this time they don't just see the person from whom they buy their groceries. They see someone's mom, or dad, or son, or daughter. They see one who has needs, joys, and hopes—a life and story outside of the box they have always seen them in. In other words, they realize that he or she is more than just the person at the grocery store checkout lane. Or perhaps they see one of their closest coworkers, but this time they see him or her with "spiritual eyes."

In response, participants in the "What do you see?" campaign simply note what God puts on their heart. Or, as God leads, they say an encouraging word or ask a thoughtful question. They may start a conversation that opens up the space—then or later—to talk more deeply about their life including the spiritual side of their life.

Finally, participants share with one another (in person if in a small group or evangelism class or online such as in a private Facebook group or other platform) what they saw and what happened next. There are always great stories to hear that grow everyone's heart for others, confidence in God, and faith that He wants to use them in others' lives.

We send the text once a day at the top of one of the hours in the participants' day—typically between 8 a.m. and 8 p.m. However, you might choose different start and end times depending on the availability and typical life patterns of the participants in your campaign. The time we send the text changes every day, and that is what makes the campaign so fun and engaging. The participants have no idea when they are going to receive it.

To accomplish this, we currently send the texts via email that we schedule ahead of time using an app like Boomerang. (Most cellphone companies allow you to send messages via email that arrive as texts. You can learn online how to do this. It's simple.) You can schedule every text for the whole campaign before the campaign begins. Doing so removes the work of sending out multiple (maybe many) individual texts every day of the campaign. Plus, you as the campaign coordinator can be surprised by the texts' arrival too.

Typically, our campaigns run for four to six weeks. For 28–42 days, participants are pausing once a day—every day—to notice the person in front of them and to see them the same way Jesus does. In addition, because participants don't know when the text will arrive, they anticipate receiving it at the top of every hour especially if the text arrives later in the day. If they receive the text earlier in the day, its impact shapes the rest of their day. In other words, participants aren't just thinking about seeing others the way Jesus does once a day, but throughout the whole day. Over time, the habit forms and participants increasingly become *sent ones* who regularly notice others and see them the same way Jesus does.

I want to encourage each of us to take part in a "What Do You See?" campaign at least once. If we were to do so, I truly believe that we would increasingly step into wonderful opportunities to bless and into great gospel conversations that we would otherwise miss—connections like I almost missed with my neighbor Bill.

A few days after Bill and I talked on my street for the first time, we met for coffee. It was a really special time. I learned that Bill enjoyed a highly successful career as a business executive. He helped shape the computer industry that we all enjoy today. I could listen to the stories he has since told me time and time again. I also learned that his wife was terminally ill and had been living in a skilled nursing facility for five years. He spent several hours a day, every day, by her bedside and kept to a certain schedule while walking Scout. That's why I saw him at the same time every day back in our neighborhood.

Bill learned that I was in full-time ministry and had just begun my new role with Cru as the national director of grad ministry. He was instantly interested in my role with Cru and generously asked questions and offered advice. But most significantly, he opened up about his interest in God and about his desire to know Him.

We agreed to meet again and have been meeting in that same coffee shop for over four years. At times there have been long stretches in between but we've easily picked up where we left off. Bill has now become one of my dearest friends. He's cheered me on and offered really helpful advice as

Bill and I are now studying Scripture regarding what it means to walk with Christ as a believer. If he hasn't already, he is extremely close to receiving Christ into his life.

I seek to lead grad ministry nationally for Cru. I've cheered him on and talked through every question he has had on his journey to faith in Christ. And nearly every time, we talk about his next big trip (his last continent to visit is Antarctica, and he is currently working on the details for that) and the latest technological advances he's following.

Since we met, Bill's wife has passed away, as has his sweet dog Scout. But he has crafted a vibrant network of friends which I am blessed to be a part of. And he has become a good friend of my family. He even joined my family for Christmas Eve service and our Christmas Eve dinner.

Through it all, God has faithfully, continually, and powerfully drawn Bill to Himself. He read through *The Case for Christ* by Lee Strobel and shared copies of it with several of his friends. I have clearly explained the gospel to him multiple times using the booklet *Knowing God Personally*. We are now studying Scripture regarding what it means to walk with Christ as a believer. If he hasn't already, he is extremely close to receiving Christ into his life.

And it almost all never took place. He almost kept being only that man who walks his dog every day by my house whose name I didn't even know.

May God give us His eyes so that we can be *sent ones* who see His people His way.

YOUR SENT LIFE

Consider / Discuss

1. Have you ever felt so distracted that you don't notice the people around you?

2. What prevents you and most people from really seeing the people around us?

3. Do you think, in general, that people have become more and more isolated from being around people?

4. What do you think of Jesus' command to "Look, I tell you, lift up your eyes, and see that the fields are white for harvest" in John 4:35?

Steps of Faith:

1. Begin your first *What do you see?* campaign with a group of friends or even for your larger church community. Gather phone numbers and choose which program you'll use to send randomized text messages over a four- to six-week period. At the time of this writing, we've used the Boomerang app, but other scheduling services exist you can try.

2. Take a step of faith to ask about the person present with you when the text message arrives.

3. If the text arrives and you aren't near anyone, consider praying for a person on your list of five people.

4. Record what happens when your *What do you see?* texts come in.

CHAPTER 7

Gathering and Caring

They broke bread in their homes and ate together with glad
and sincere hearts, praising God and enjoying the favor of
all the people. And the Lord added to their number daily
those who were being saved.

—Acts 2:46–47

Only around half of Americans (53 percent) have meaningful in-person social interactions, such as having an extended
conversation with a friend or spending quality time
with family, on a daily basis.

—2018 Cigna National Survey on Loneliness

W e invited you here because we're all *lonely*. I'm lonely. I
don't see anyone in the neighborhood anymore. So that's
why we invited you here tonight," I (Heather) said as I cut thick
slices of homemade bread one Monday evening in January.

The fragrance of a warm soup—an African Peanut Stew, vegan
and gluten free to accommodate those around the table—wafted

from the big white bowls I bought at a bargain from Target. I baked
a loaf of sourdough potato bread that my friend Jan taught me how
to make last summer. Ashley tossed a salad and filled the water
glasses. This was our "Soup and Stories" night we would host every
other Monday night.

The concept was simple, but we prayed for two years to figure
it out. We wanted to design a way to gather the neighbors together
in our unique stage of life. For years, I knew how to do this as a
mom with elementary-aged children, but how would we gather
couples with older teens and busy professional lives? Nobody had
time for any kind of socializing. And in our own family, even having family dinner felt like managing the chaos of conflicting teen
work schedules, youth group, marching band, or school projects.

But one evening, I realized that every person *needs to eat*.
What if I simply made a big pot of soup right during the work week
and asked neighbors to pop in, eat their soup, and be on their way?
They would inevitably ask, "What can I bring?" and I'd say, "Noth-
ing but a story about your day—nothing but a story." That's how
"Soup and Stories" began.

Neighbors came straight from work—covered with sawdust
from their woodworking shop, in hospital scrubs, or in professional
clothes from their campus office—and they'd sit down to take a
moment to share a steaming bowl of soup and some warm bread.

I'll never forget that first night. As I finished telling everyone
about our loneliness and disconnection from each other and my
belief in the power of storytelling, the first neighbor nodded and
said, "We should all go around the table and share either a breakdown, a breakthrough, or a breakup from our day. I'll go first. I'm
having a breakdown!" She burst into tears right then, and we all
cared for her and entered into her story.

A year later, we were still gathering to share our stories of *break-downs, breakthroughs, and breakups.* My husband and I speak freely about Jesus as we tell of our spiritual challenges (our breakdowns), our insights from Scripture (our breakthroughs), or anything we've had to end in order to walk closely with Jesus (our breakups). We pray before we eat and ask God to bless each neighbor.

As the weeks passed, Ashley and I remembered *we were sent to this exact neighborhood* to bless and minister. Living a sent life meant—and continues to mean—asking God how we can gather and care for the people right around us and create the space for ongoing spiritual conversations. On Monday nights, our Soup and Stories has become a precious and deeply treasured time for all. I've learned the joy of blessing others with food around the table, and my repertoire of delicious soups has expanded to include a hearty 16-Bean, Coconut Thai Carrot, Potato Leak, Corn Chowder, and a spicy Mexican.

Last Monday night as I chopped vegetables for the big stew-pot, I recalled another time in my life several years earlier when the neighbors also gathered on Monday nights. What started as a simple exercise initiative blossomed into something I never imag-ined would have the scope of impact that it did, as I'll share shortly.

--------- ✳ ---------

As I've written before in *Seated with Christ: Living Freely in a Culture of Comparison,*[1] the Lord reminded me that He chose me for this exact neighborhood, and I changed my daily schedule in order to make myself available to the people God put in my natu-ral pathways. But just as the three core principles guided my sent life—God is at work to draw people to Himself; He uses us to lead others to Jesus; and He continually invites us into the work of evangelism—I developed the life-changing conviction that God left me placed right here out of His sovereign plan to build His kingdom. He left me here. I'm still here because of the work left to do. I'm here because God has chosen this location (Acts 17), and every interaction now filters through this lens of being sent to minister to the people around me. It's the same for you, too.

For me, it all began with a phone call to invite parents and children to join our family for a Neighborhood Fitness Night. That night after dinner, I went into the front yard with jump ropes and bikes. All of a sudden, I saw them coming. Family after family arrived on the front lawn to play. As the children raced around (with me timing them with a stopwatch for various races; and I coordinated vintage games like Red-Light-Green-Light and Mother May I?), the adults shook hands and talked. We decided right then and there to have neighborhood fitness night every week—even every night if we could.

When it grew too dark, we moved our fitness time up. When our group became too large, we moved to the school parking lot, and sometimes up to fifty people came to exercise. When it got too cold, we moved our neighborhood fitness group into our basement for Monday night fitness group.

For five years, we met in our basement during the winter for one hour after dinner for dancing, jumping jacks, and whatever fitness activity we could invent. We challenged each other to jump rope one hundred times, do one hundred jumping jacks, and dance for twenty minutes without stopping. The local news came out to cover our Neighborhood Fitness Group. I even have a letter from the White House, signed by Michelle Obama, thanking our neighborhood for our commitment to healthy living.

One night, a couple said to me, "We've lived in our home for four years, and you were the first neighbor to invite us anywhere."

Seven years later, I had walked over 2,500 miles with my neighbors. In addition to walking, Ashley and I began hosting pancake breakfasts for the neighbors. Besides this, I discovered fellow writers around me, and these neighbors soon gathered for writing groups. My husband invited the men for a night out, too. As our neighbors gathered, we also accomplished multiple service projects for schools, churches, and shelters, and offered support and care for hurting people.

Most significant, at least seven people prayed to receive Christ in our one-mile radius. My ministry philosophy was quite simple but profound: *I spoke to people as if they were already believers.* I told my stories of how Jesus has transformed my life. I entered into natural spiritual conversations based on what I was learning in the Bible.

A neighbor who followed the Hindu tradition wanted to hear everything I had to say about Jesus. When she understood the gospel and the free gift of salvation, she couldn't believe that Jesus claimed to forgive sin. No other religion offered her that. She also couldn't believe that she didn't have to pay anything for this salvation since Jesus paid the price to save her. When she prayed to receive Christ into her life, she not only led her husband and two children to Jesus, but she also has a thriving neighborhood and campus ministry of her own today. And it all began with calling neighbors to gather for some exercise.

———————————*———————————

In March of 2020, Ashley and I—like the rest of the world—found ourselves in a new COVID-19 reality. Coffee dates, neighborhood get-togethers, and campus gatherings were all shut down, but we still understood the power of gathering people together whether through Zoom invitations, neighborhood Facebook groups, or a daily walk with a couple where we practiced the recommended six-foot distancing as we walked. In many ways, gathering became easier, not harder. Virtual gathering became vital for our well-being and sense of connection. We hosted Soup and Stories on a Zoom call where we all ate dinner together online and shared stories. Ashley invited Bill to "phone call discipleship." I texted colleagues to check in on them and asked for prayer requests with a boldness and concern I had never felt before. Ashley walked up and down our street and called out for neighbors to email him their information to join a Facebook group for neighbors to share concerns and news. We realized that even though we were being asked to "socially distance," the real protocol was only physical distance. In fact, more than ever, we found ourselves moving toward others with love and care—just at a safe distance. And we saw God open up the door for several fresh spiritual conversations.

Harvard research has declared an epidemic of loneliness in our culture, and this trend has only increased.[2] A 2018 research study by the global health service company Cigna revealed alarming results that make our sent calling all the more timely and vital. In a survey of over 20,000 adults in the US, nearly half reported "always feeling alone," while one in four Americans claimed that they "never feel as though there are people who really understand them." Even worse, two in five adults say they "always feel that their relationships are not meaningful" and as many surveyed claimed they "are isolated from others." Half of US adults claimed they do not have "meaningful in-person social interactions" and do not have quality time or extended conversations with others on a daily basis. The Cigna survey, while troubling, offers hope for our mission. The researchers conclude this:

> The survey also revealed several important bright spots. The findings reinforce the social nature of humans and the importance of having communities. People who are less lonely are more likely to have regular, meaningful, in-person interactions; are in good overall physical and mental health; have achieved balance in daily activities; and are employed and have good relationships with their coworkers. [3]

As we gather people together in communities, we increase the likelihood of gospel conversations and we solve a significant crisis in our world. So hungry are lonely people for community, however, that they will find it wherever they can. This urges Christians in particular to understand why we see the rise of so many pseudo-religious groups that replace what the traditional church once was in the community.

In fact, a recent Harvard research study titled "How We Gather" noted that many non-religious organizations gather members based on six qualities "historically associated with faith gatherings: community, personal transformation, social transformation, purpose finding, creativity, and accountability."[4] The study explains, according to Barna's analysis, why people look to groups like CrossFit or SoulCycle "to play the role traditionally reserved for religious community."[5]

People desire things like community, transformation, and purpose, which explains how in just one neighborhood, three programs took root and blossomed: Neighborhood Fitness, the Walk-to-School Campaign, and Soup and Stories.

But what about your community? As you think about gathering others together, consider two key questions:

What are the physical or emotional needs of those around you?
What are the primary interests of those around you?

As you brainstorm what you believe people most need around you, consider forming a weekly group to meet that need whether centered on exercise, food, connection, or even some kind of training in parenting, marriage, or finances. Back in graduate school, the need I saw involved supporting others to finish their dissertations and enjoy weekly encouragement in a culture of complaint and criticism.

In 1999, I began the Encouragement Group—a weekly gathering of PhD candidates who met at a café each week. We talked about our research and writing, and we all encouraged one another and celebrated as we met personal goals. We journeyed alongside someone training for a marathon, for example, and another who needed encouragement in her relationships. For years we met every week. Twenty years later, we reunited and still gather via Google Hangouts to have a monthly Encouragement Group. I share Scripture, pray blessings over the members, and wait for an open door to share the gospel.

Next, consider the *primary interests* of those around you. In all my years of community building, I've learned it deeply matters when you simply care about the hobbies of others. In my own life and ministry, I've learned the power of entering into the interests of others, even when at first I had no desire to join in. You may find yourself entering into the world of sports, woodworking, music, hiking, or baking. As you learn about the people around you, simply ask if you might join them one day in what they love doing.

One funny way I've joined into the interests of others involves the dogs in my neighborhood. So many people adored their dogs and walked them down the sidewalks that I decided to walk too. I'd carry dog treats in my pockets and ask if I could give their dogs a treat. I don't have dogs—I'm a cat person!—but living a sent life means I love the people and the pets around me.

As Ashley and I led our church course on living a sent life, we encouraged each participant to step out in faith and attempt to gather others. We include this account below of a woman who had lived in her community for years without ever meeting her neighbors:

It started with the "awkward bread encounters."

My husband, Dave, and I participated in an evangelism class at our church, and one of our assignments was to think about how we might reach out to our neighbors. The guidelines were specific: this was not to be a grand, reach-out-to-the-world type of evangelism. Instead, we were asked to think about a truly local, targeted invitation to form relationships with folks near our homes.

My first attempt at this began with small loaves of homemade bread.

My mother taught me how to make bread when I was a little girl. Breadmaking is as natural to me as walking, so I thought it seemed an obvious pathway to fulfill our class assignment: make bread and share loaves with the nearest neighbors—next door and across the street—a total of four homes.

I've known all these houses for as long as I can remember, but I found myself somewhat embarrassed that I didn't know the names of all the people living there.

I started my get-to-know-the-neighbors breadmaking on a lovely July day, warm and sunny, perfect for allowing yeast to rise. As I made the bread, mixing, kneading, letting it rise, punching down, letting it rise again, and baking, I noticed that I'd added a new ingredient to my bread recipe: uncertainty.

The loaves baked as usual, and I made four baskets of warm, aromatic bread and added to each basket a jar of homemade jelly. Still feeling an uncommon uncertainty, I set out the front door, making four short individual trips to the two houses on either side and the two houses directly across the street. The receptions to my bread and jelly baskets were somewhat varying, but had a common theme: each encounter was awkward. I just sort of self-consciously proffered the baskets, mumbled a few uncomfortable words, and fled. All in all, not a wonderfully successful effort!

There was one positive reaction. A few days later I found an overflowing basket of fresh garden vegetables on our front porch. One of the bread recipients had put together a bounty from her beautiful garden and had left the gift for us. It was a kind and hospitable act, and it touched me deeply that she had been moved to such a friendly effort.

The next week at our Sunday evening class at church, I relayed my dismal "awkward bread" effort to the teachers and classmates. There was laughter and empathy, as well as gentle counsel to keep trying. This led me back to the drawing board. I began the next effort not by thinking or brainstorming, but with prayer. I asked God to direct me on a Spirit-led undertaking to invite my neighbors into my home, and to get to know them at a real and personal level.

Sometime during the next week, God led me to the idea of a neighborhood women's book club. I'd had a wonderful experience in a book club for many years in a different city. It had been such a good experience that a new book club seemed like a perfect fit for our evangelism class assignment.

I took a long morning to work on an invitation, praying and writing and rewriting. I didn't intend this to be a Christian book club. The point was not to preach or proselytize, but rather simply to make genuine connections with my neighbors. I finally came up with an invitation that seemed about right, printed out twenty-five copies, and walked around delivering them. I figured if two or three people responded, it would be a successful outcome.

Within hours, my phone began to ring. Over the span of the next day, twenty neighbors responded in the affirmative. And the response was not a mild, milquetoast "yes"; it was, across-the-board, a delighted "YES!" I found that we had tapped into a deep and abiding need, a desire to connect on more than a superficial level with one another.

We had the first meeting within a few weeks, and it turned into a satisfying evening. Starting with simply sharing our names, we soon were sharing food and drinks, backgrounds, and experiences. As the evening progressed, we agreed to a few simple rules: we would meet once a month, circulate locations and hostesses, pick books based on a consensus vote; and come even if you hadn't read the book.

The point from the beginning was clearly not only about books; it was and still is about connections.

That was a year ago. The club has solidified into a membership of about a dozen or so consistent members, but we often have a guest or a new interested person drop in. We come from different backgrounds, beliefs, interests. We have read books across the spectrum—fiction and nonfiction, light and heavy, secular and religious. The discussions are lively and insightful. We challenge ourselves and each other, and we also simply enjoy our time together.

More than that, we have developed deeper connections outside the book club. For example, we supported a member who had an unexpected surgery with a schedule of meals for a couple weeks, we found a car seat for a member with visiting grandchildren, we helped find outlets for housekeeping goods donated by another. We widened the girlfriend relationships to include a few dinners as couples' dinners, and some of the husbands and other family members have also gotten to know one another.

We do not know how this book club will develop, but we know it will continue. We have had the incredibly lovely experience of simply enjoying our discussions and each other. Our club has been, and will continue to be, an incredible gift.

As I spoke with this friend recently, she shared how God continues to work in this book club and how God has even provided opportunities to talk more specifically about her relationship with Jesus—even to the point of giving a Bible to a curious friend. We marveled at how she took a step of faith and how God blessed her efforts.

We'll now challenge you to the same challenge we give our Sent class: How might you gather people together this week?

YOUR SENT LIFE

Consider / Discuss

1. What's happening in the culture around you that prevents others from gathering together?

2. Think about the primary physical and emotional needs in the people surrounding your home, workplace, or in your natural pathways (where you spend time each day).

3. What hobbies would you like to develop (or have developed) that you could invite others to join you in?

4. What hobbies do you observe in the lives of others around you?

Steps of Faith:

1. Begin praying about a way you might gather people together.

2. Send out invitations to this first gathering.

3. Invite a few other people to enter into a hobby or interest of yours.

4. Discover the hobbies of two to five friends in your life. Ask them if you might join them in their hobby or interest sometime in the next month.

CHAPTER 8

The Easiest Questions to Ask

Don't look out only for your own interests,
but take an interest in others, too.

—Paul in Philippians 2:4 NLT

If I (Heather) could pick the essential character trait I wish followers of Christ would develop more, I'd choose that of *curiosity*. In fact, I pray this for my children. I also talk to both my undergraduate and graduate students about developing curiosity as a key professional skill. In particular, I mean *social or interpersonal curiosity*—the desire to know and understand more about other people.

I read and think about curiosity because I've learned that people who don't desire to engage others about their lives—even at the most basic level of interest—will hardly desire to talk with them about deeper spiritual issues. But just as evangelism is so good for your relationship with Jesus—and so fun and joyful, building curiosity isn't something to put on your to-do list that makes you feel a sense of shame or drudgery. In fact, the practice of simply being curious about other people enhances intimacy, well-being, and happiness. Yet, like evangelism, we often shy away from asking others about their lives because we feel it's rude or awkward. Or we don't know how. Or worse, we're just self-absorbed.

Can we develop the trait of curiosity as a prerequisite to vital spiritual conversations? What is curiosity anyway? Living a sent life means we're *curious about others as a way to build connection that leads to gospel conversations.*

If you scan the research articles in both psychology, social science, and neuroscience, you'll learn about both the scope and benefits of becoming a curious person. Todd Kashdan, a leading researcher on curiosity, explains curiosity like this:

> Curiosity's immediate function is to seek out, explore, and immerse oneself in situations with potential for new information and/or experiences. In the longer term, consistently acting on curious feelings functions to expand knowledge, build competencies, strengthen social relationships, and increase intellectual and creative capacities.[1]

Essentially, curious people desire new information about others; they believe they will learn something important or meaningful. But how does one develop curiosity? How do we leave our homes to engage well with others about their lives?

Curiosity, I'm learning, reflects a way to love others well and care about their lives. Socially curious people love learning about others because they hold a posture of high regard for them; their desire to learn more about others dignifies them and imagines them hiding rich treasures of experiences, insights, and wisdom. When we allow ourselves to feel curious about other people's lives, we essentially believe that we will discover something meaningful and valuable from this interaction.

Additionally, a curious heart is a humble, teachable heart. It's a heart set on discovering more about the person before them who is made in the very image of God. Even more, curiosity is a state of being fully present with a person, what Dr. Kashdan calls "mindful immersion."[2]

When we're curious about others, it's a way of associating with them and believing they have something to teach us. Consider Paul's command in Romans 12:16: "Live in harmony with one another. Do not be proud, but be willing to associate with people of low position. Do not be conceited." Consider, too, the virtue of learning about others and showing interest in their lives as a way of being devoted to one another and honoring "one another above yourselves" (Rom.12:10). As Paul talks about imitating Christ's love in Philippians 2, he tells us clearly in verse 4: "Don't look out only for your own interests, but take an interest in others, too" (NLT). As I think about how to cultivate a heart that truly takes an interest in others, I find the research on curiosity so helpful to motivate us to learn more about this overlooked but powerful part of our sent identity. We might seek, as Kashdan urges, to make curiosity "a fundamental part of our lives."[3]

But why? Aside from the biblical mandate to take an interest in other people, as it turns out, curious people maintain "high levels of well-being and meaning in life."[4] And, as reported from UC Berkeley in an article titled "Why Curious People Have Better Relationships," we read this gem of a statement: "Being interested is more important in cultivating a relationship and maintaining a relationship than being interesting; that's what gets the dialogue going. It's the secret juice of relationships."[5] Additionally, curiosity is in itself an "intrinsically pleasurable experience."[6] When you're curious, you're less socially anxious, critical, and even less aggressive.[7] I've also heard someone tell me, "It's hard to be mad and curious at the same time."

Curiosity about others blesses them. And it blesses you.

---※---

I recently asked my teenage daughter if she has any friends who ask her about her life and seem to care about what happens to her. She talks about how rare this is, how nobody ever asks her questions about her life, and how, in a school of over 2,500 teens, she could only name *one person* who asks her personal questions. And this one friend, with her loving questions, makes my daughter feel cared for.

What does it mean to feel cared for by others? In a recent Barna study of 15,000 people surveyed, only a third of young adults surveyed feel cared for by others.[8] Curiosity about people's lives show we care about them. I surveyed friends and family to discover that rarely will others ask them questions about their lives. When they get together with friends, besides talking about the news or the weather or simply monologuing about work or children, rarely will someone ask a good question about their lives. It leaves so many of us frustrated, isolated, and empty after spending a significant amount of time in meaningless interaction.

When was the last time you felt truly cared for because of the questions someone asked you about your life? When was the last time you felt that another person was looking out for your interests, wanting you to succeed, and figuring out ways to personally encourage you?

We stand poised for a cultural revolution of loving curiosity about others that positions us to enter into meaningful conversations that lead to spiritual topics.

Curiosity in Practice

Since curiosity fuels creativity and joy—not only in families and communities but also in the workplace—business leaders have taken a great interest in how to cultivate a posture of curiosity. One business leader reports how a colleague began her journey toward living in curiosity. She began to ask herself this question: "What would I say *if* I were curious?" This single question helped people build their curiosity.[9]

It's a great technique to try: Simply enter a conversation and let your mind role-play what a curious person would ask. Imagine you're a curious person who loves gathering information about others for the pure joy of understanding their lives and how God designed them. Imagine this curiosity leads to awe and worship as you discover the complexity of another person. And imagine how curiosity will bless this person. What kinds of questions bless others and invite them to open up their lives to us?

At Penn State, I'm known for my "Name Games" and the English department passes around my list of seventy questions designed to help foster community in my writing workshops. The Name Games formed over the last two decades of teaching; I needed an easy way to help me connect with my students and allow them to connect with one another. I ask students to tell everyone their name and then answer a single question. After years of asking "What would you like to know about each other today?" my list grew and included everything from questions like, "What's your favorite quote?" to "What was the first song you listened to over and over again?"

However, one question far surpasses them all as a way to immediately enter into a loving conversation with another person. This single question has fostered more community than any other I've ever asked before. It's this:

What question do you wish people would ask you about yourself?

I learned the power of this question on a winter day during my morning writing class. I told the class we'd all go around the room and answer this question. Hopefully, we'd remember how others answered, and we'd remember later when we saw them in the dining hall or in a coffee shop or even at a party. One basketball player immediately raised his hand. "I'll go first," he insisted. And then he said, "I hate it when everyone only asks me about basketball. I don't want to talk about basketball, but that's the only thing people ask me about." He paused and looked around the room.

"What do you wish people would ask you about yourself?" I prompted.

"I wish people would ask me about the video game I play. I'm really good. I love talking about it." The girl sitting beside him immediately asked about the game, and he smiled.

> *I simply said to my neighbor, "I'm a Christian, and I'm so curious: What does your tradition say about Jesus?"*

"My boyfriend plays that game. He knows who you are. I should play with you both," she offered.

Next, a student called out, "I wish people would ask me about the screenplay I'm writing." Another cried, "Nobody asks me about my dog, and I miss her so much!" Others wanted us to ask them about the movies they love, the classes that fascinate them, or what sports team they follow.

I encouraged students that on their first dates or when meeting a new friend, simply say, "Hey, I want to get to know you better. What question do you like people to ask you?"

I tried the technique during a wedding reception when my husband and I were seated at a round table. We introduced ourselves around the table and answered the question. We learned the names of these new friends and how one wanted us to ask her about growing up on a dairy farm; another wanted us to inquire about the home gym he built. Still another wanted us to ask him about his current goals.

Last Thanksgiving, I invited my extended family to answer the question, and for the first time in my life, I learned that my own father wished we'd ask him about his fountain pen collection and that my brother-in-law enjoys when people ask his opinion about important topics in the news.

I can think of no better loving question for a new friend: "What question do you like people to ask you?"

———— ⋈ ————

Now primed for true connection, sent people naturally move into spiritual conversation easily. As I train others in evangelism practices, I suggest what I call the Four Best Questions:

THE FOUR BEST QUESTIONS

1. What does your tradition say about Jesus?
2. Do you consider yourself on a spiritual journey? What is that like? Where are you on that journey?
3. I'm in a fresh season of prayer. Do you have any prayer requests I might commit to pray for?
4. Can I tell you something I just learned in the Bible that's changing how I handle _____?

During one of the many walks to school in the morning, I simply said to my neighbor, "I'm a Christian, and I'm so curious: What does your tradition say about Jesus?" That single curious question opened up a dialogue and set her on a path to discover Jesus for herself. My friend reports the impact of the question like this:

> Her question was, "What does your tradition say about Jesus?"
>
> That question really got me thinking. I started questioning, "Where is this path [I'm on] going?" Raising this question, "Who is Jesus?"—that just sparked something in me. I started reading the book of John. At the same time, I went to my [spiritual books]—I had plenty of those, so I was like, "What do these say about Jesus? What do they say about the one true path?"
>
> That was the question I kept coming back to. I was praying to Him, saying, "Jesus, are you the Way, the Truth, and the Life? You have to tell me!" Then I would go to my [New Age] prayers and pray in that direction. [I thought] *Who is telling the truth here?*

The main thing that was missing that kept me coming back to Jesus was this: Where is the provision for sin? I just had nowhere to take my sins. And they were weighing me down. There was no place to go with that. There was no place to say, "Who is going to forgive me?"[10]

As my friend struggled and wondered over this question "Who is Jesus?" and as she read the Bible, she came to understand that Jesus was her Savior and the one true God. She explains this:

I literally turned, and it was like I smacked right into [Jesus]. It was like He was right there waiting for me . . . I remember having this moment—and I still have this photo—where I had my cellphone and I just took a picture of myself because I wanted to remember this day. There's just a lightness and a freedom now that comes from praying to Him, surrendering to Him, and praying with other people in His name.[11]

Later in her journey with Jesus, my friend quoted to me her now favorite Bible verse: "These are written that you may believe that Jesus is the Messiah, the Son of God, and that by believing you may have life in his name" (John 20:31).

The second curious question often happens in my office hours at Penn State, especially if I find a student in distress, a faculty member struggling with a personal issue, or a graduate student popping in for advice. I'll pause and say, "You know, I'm wondering something. These seem like spiritual problems we're talking about. Do you consider yourself on a spiritual journey?" As a person answers my question, it inevitably leads to an opportunity to share my own spiritual journey of becoming a Christ follower.

The third question involves asking people how you can pray for them. I've never once had a person turn down my offer to add them to my prayer journal. In fact, when a student told me about her chronic pain and upcoming surgery, I told her I would indeed pray for her. Her eyes filled with tears. As she sat in my office, she said, "I think this is the nicest thing anyone has ever said to me."

Sometimes, when I'm with a group of people who ask how I'm doing, I'll say, "I'm learning so much about prayer and I keep a detailed prayer journal. Do you all have any prayer requests?" Mostly people ask about this idea of a "prayer journal," and I have the opportunity to talk about writing down specific prayers and then recording how the Lord answers them. I often share from Psalm 5:3 where David writes, "In the morning, LORD, you hear my voice; in the morning I lay my requests before you and wait expectantly." I'll share that Christians believe that, because of Jesus' sacrifice for our sin, we can approach God confidently to find help in our time of need (Heb. 4:16) and that God is our "ever-present help in trouble" (Ps. 46:1).

Finally, you might enter into conversations by sharing your own story of transformation. When I'm in a situation where people share about fear or anxiety, it's so easy to say, "I found something in the Bible that's really helping me deal with this. Can I tell you about it?" Even a former atheist colleague stopping by my office would ask how God helped me conquer my fear of public speaking or travel anxiety. In the next chapter, you'll learn more about how to tell stories of transformation to engage your family, neighbors, and coworkers.

After you've used any of the four questions, you might consider this last easy question to ask to talk about Jesus. You might say, "You can probably tell I'm a Christian and someone who studies the Bible. I love to talk about my faith. Do you happen to have any questions about Jesus I could answer for you?" Sometimes people just need an invitation to express their own curious questions.

I recently heard the story of a new friend who sat by a Muslim woman on a plane. My friend simply asked if she was Muslim and the conversation took off. My friend listened to her describe what Islam meant to her. When my friend said, "Well, I'm a Christian, and I'm wondering this: Do you have any questions for me about Jesus?" the woman said, "Yes! I do! I wonder how anyone would know which religion was really true. How do I know what truth is?"

I think of that woman on a plane whose heart had questions like this but no one to ask. Since my friend knew that both she and her Muslim friend were arriving to the same city, she invited her and her husband to dinner to talk about Jesus' claim in John 14:6, where He says, "I am the way and the truth and the life. No one comes to the Father except through me." My friend said, "I will share with you why Jesus said He is the truth."

Sometimes, we must open the space to invite people to ask their questions about Jesus. We cultivate their curiosity as we work on building our own. As you begin practicing living as a sent person, growing a curious heart will deeply bless those around you. Simply begin by saying, "I'm so curious about you—tell me about *you*. What question do you like people to ask you?" Soon, you'll feel like you're living out the command in Romans 12:10 where Paul says, "Be devoted to one another in love. Honor one another above yourselves."

YOUR SENT LIFE

Consider / Discuss

1. Think about a person who showed genuine interest in your life by asking good questions. What questions did they ask you?

2. What does it mean to take an interest in others?

3. What do you think curious people believe about others that makes them interested in their lives? In other words, what motivates curiosity?

4. Why do you think curiosity matters for living a sent life?

Steps of Faith:

1. Identify a few people in your life on whom you might practice the art of curiosity. Think of a few questions to ask them. Eventually, take a step of faith to ask a person either what their spiritual tradition says about Jesus or whether they consider themselves on a spiritual journey.

2. Ask a friend what question he or she wishes you would ask them.

3. Write a few sentences to characterize how a curious person acts and what it might look like to be devoted to others. What most needs to change in your life to show your curiosity and devotion to others?

4. Take note of how you feel after a week of being curious about others. Did Kashdan's research about curiosity become true for you in terms of your own well-being?

CHAPTER 9

The Easiest Story to Tell

[Stories] are the most effective form of human communication, more powerful than any other way of packaging information. And telling purposeful stories is certainly the most efficient means of persuasion in everyday life, the most effective way of translating ideas into action.

—CEO of Mandalay Entertainment
and Producer Peter Guber

Every fall semester at Penn State, just as the crisp morning air and red-tipped oak leaves promise a beautiful Pennsylvania autumn, I invite a new class of writing students to tell me their *Signature Stories*. The Signature Story, according to a professor of marketing at Stanford (who popularized the term "signature story" for the business world), defines this kind of story as a personal narrative you leverage to advocate for an idea; it's "an intriguing, authentic, involving narrative with a strategic message."[1]

I stand in front of my students, in a typical brown cardigan, burgundy glasses, and thermos of coffee with hazelnut creamer, and I ask, "What's the story you tell everyone about your life?

What moments shape who you are, your call to a vocation, or why you care about certain ideas?" Students use these stories in their professional portfolios and on their websites to move people to action regarding various philanthropic causes. They come to realize the unmatched power of storytelling as the "most effective form of human communication."[2]

One of the most powerful tools we possess is the ability to communicate our stories of transformation to showcase God at work. I often consider, too, how your unique stories—orchestrated by God who positions us right where we are—intersect with the lives of others as we tell our stories.

A story you tell of your personal transformation in Christ might serve as the exact narrative to reach the heart of a person God has put in your path. Your story might be for *them* and only you can tell it just because of who you are.

Therapist and writer Mary Pipher, in her book *Writing to Change the World,* writes this:

> You have something to say that no one else can say. Your history, your unique sensibilities, your sense of place, and your language bestow upon you a singular authority. Who but you can describe the hollyhocks in your grandmother's backyard, or the creek outside of town that you fished as a child . . .[3]

Living a sent life means God sends you with stories to tell. Consider 1 Peter 2:9 and how you are "chosen people" in order to "declare the praises of him who called you out of darkness into his wonderful light." You have stories of coming out of darkness that only you can tell. And when you tell these stories to others, they engage with you differently from when you tell them facts or arguments. God made our brains to enjoy story.

Recent neuroscience tells us what happens to your brain as you hear a story. Professor of Neurology Paul Zak recently published his findings on the neuroscience of narrative, and his conclusions confirm something vital for living a sent life. Dr. Zak and his research team explain how when the brain receives a story, it releases cortisol (attention, stress) and oxytocin (empathy, connection) that affect behavior and drive personal transformation in ways that facts do not.[4]

When you begin to tell a story to someone, they therefore listen more attentively and bond with you; they inhabit the story as they listen for what's going to happen next. Business leader Nancy Duarte explains why we need stories; she insists the brain is "hardwired" to enjoy transformation.[5]

As filmmaker Peter Guber claims, "Telling stories is not just the oldest form of entertainment, it's the highest form of consciousness. The need for narrative is embedded deep in our brains. Increasingly, success in the information age demands that we harness the hidden power of stories."[6]

As a professor of rhetoric (the art of persuasion) and as a person living a sent life, I care deeply about what it means to communicate the message of the gospel well. I tend to think about logical arguments, a clear refutation of opposing claims, and all the ways I can argue with strong reasoning. But Guber reminds me what so many ancient scholars from Cicero to Aristotle remind us: facts don't *persuade*. They don't move people to action. Guber concludes this:

Reams of data rarely engage people to move them to action. Stories, on the other hand, are state-of-the-*heart* technology—they connect us to others. They provide emotional transportation, moving people to take action on your cause because they can very quickly come to psychologically identify with the characters in a narrative or share an experience—courtesy of the images evoked in the telling.[7]

Guber's statements help me understand why Jesus chose to teach in parables—short, memorable stories used to illustrate a spiritual truth—instead of only presenting Scripture or argument.

If our personal stories of gospel transformation are our most critical asset, how do we tell our personal stories well? I teach my students that every good life story is "shaped by three critical elements—a challenge, struggle, and some resolution."[8] As you read this chapter, consider your three most important life stories involving the Lord's work in your life—perhaps your salvation story, a surrender story, and a story of miraculous blessing or answer to prayer. Think about yourself as a character in a setting who has a "before" experience, the "during" experience, and the "after" experience. As you write this story, remember to include sensory detail (include the five senses: sights, sounds, textures, tastes, smells), perhaps the time of day, and yourself as an actual character in a story. As you let the Lord bring key stories to mind, think about the biblical invitation to tell your stories.

Recently, I explored the number of times Scripture invites us to tell our story. Consider these prompts. In Psalm 107:2, the psalmist writes, "Let the redeemed of the LORD *tell their story.*" In Psalm 66:16, the writer proclaims, "Come and hear, all you who fear God; *let me tell you* what he has done for me." In fact, throughout the psalms, you'll find a call to tell your story.

In Psalm 71:15, we read how the psalmist speaks all day long about the things the Lord has done. Can you imagine the stories of miracles, of victory, and of God's faithfulness as we read, "My mouth will tell of your righteous deeds, of your saving acts all day long—though I know not how to relate them all." We're given the model for doing so by David in Psalm 105:1–2 who says, "Give praise to the LORD, proclaim his name; make known among the nations what he has done. Sing to him, sing praise to him; tell of all his wonderful acts," which he then continues to narrate for the next thirty verses. David, it seems, has a story to tell.

Finally, the writer of Psalm 71 even asks God in verse 18 to preserve his life "till [he declares God's] power to the next generation, [His] mighty acts to all who are to come." As you gather your most significant stories of God's work in your life—through salvation, your surrender of any area of your life to Him, and the way He has provided for you—remember this powerful call to tell the next generation about the Lord.

I met with a graduate student yesterday who wanted to learn how to share her faith with those around her—including family members who had yet to know Jesus. She talked about how she didn't want to engage in controversy or start an argument (especially with her father). As a shy and more introverted person, she didn't know even where to begin to talk about Jesus with her friends and family. She also didn't understand the basics of how to lead someone to know Jesus if the opportunity arose. After sharing with her a few versions of a gospel presentation, I told her that those

Bible verses might not be where she begins, especially if in the presence of a heated argument or any kind of combative conversation.

"What if you begin with the story of God rescuing you from something—from sin, from yourself, from something else. When did you actually become a Christian?" I asked. "Have you ever told that story?"

She hadn't. So I asked her for details. *Where were you? How old were you? What do you remember about the time of day or what the room looked like? What was going on that made you need Jesus so much? Why did you cry out to Him?*

As she told her story of transformation—of God rescuing her from a toxic and dangerous relationship—she then added that it wasn't the last time she dealt with someone she trusted taking advantage of her. "And God also rescued me from that situation."

She told this next story of rescue as I listened. I began to notice a theme—just as she did—of finding someone to trust who would not fail her.

Then I answered the question she and so many others ask as they begin to write down their stories of the Lord's work in their life. "Who would listen to my story? How do I just start telling it?"

As we huddled together to walk to the bus stop with snow flurries thickening in the air, we talked about this theme of finding unfailing love, having someone to trust, and being rescued from a toxic situation. I said, "I think most people around you need to hear a story like this. You could always respond to anyone around you dealing with betrayal, a search for love, or feeling oppressed in a situation with how you surrendered your life to Jesus and found rescue and healing." We continued to talk about her story to flesh out all the sensory details we could. My final advice was to include the passage of Scripture that God most used in her life during that time. The story sets up this passage of Scripture. A story without God's Word is a good story, but it doesn't bring the same power as Scripture.

I explained that—like a farmer sowing the word and the royal priest who brings God's Word—sprinkling in those passages of Scripture is a way to cultivate the soil of the listener's heart. And God's Word can begin to work. If we consider Romans 10:17 and how faith comes through hearing the Word of God, or in 1 Thessalonians 2:13 how the Word of God is "at work," it brings a sense of order to how we tell our stories. The story of transformation you tell will hinge on a key passage of Scripture. Consider this formula for your own stories of God's work in your life.

1. *Before:* The "before scene." Where are you? What time is it? What do you look like? What are you feeling and experiencing?
2. *Struggle:* What was the problem that God needed to solve? What were you struggling with?
3. *After:* What happened when you prayed or surrendered to God? How did He begin to change you or your situation?
4. *Scripture:* What passage of Scripture can you find that best represents God's work in this story?

This last point matters deeply. Although I'm a huge advocate of the power of storytelling and have devoted much of my teaching to helping others craft their stories of transformation, I know that stories alone are not enough to bring someone to salvation. As noted by Pastor Erik Raymond, "Our stories are helpful and even moving; however, they are not powerful unto salvation like the word of God."[9]

I remember the wise words that Paul wrote to young Timothy:

> But as for you, continue in what you have learned and have
> become convinced of, because you know those from whom
> you learned it, and how from infancy you have known the
> Holy Scriptures, which are able to make you wise for salva-
> tion through faith in Christ Jesus. All Scripture is God-
> breathed and is useful for teaching, rebuking, correcting and
> training in righteousness, so that the servant of God may be
> thoroughly equipped for every good work. (2 Tim. 3:14–17).

Here, we learn the Scriptures make us "wise for salvation" and that
these God-breathed words teach, rebuke, correct, and train.

I currently regularly tell two stories of gospel transformation
that always lead to great conversation. I've written them and memorized them so I can tell them in one to three minutes. My first
story involves Jesus rescuing me from sin in college when I was a
freshman at the University of Virginia. Note the formula of the
before scene, the struggle, the after scene, and the Scripture God
used. When spoken aloud, it's only about a one-to-two-minute
story I can use whenever anyone asks me about college, loneliness,
emptiness, bad choices, or anything that leads to sharing this story
of transformation.

Story One: Rescue

I knew I needed rescue February of my freshman year at the
University of Virginia. I was making a mess of my life by dating the wrong boys, drinking at fraternity parties, and exhausting myself trying to have the perfect grades and the perfect
skinny figure. One morning, I sat crying in my dorm room

with my brown hair matting my face. I was so depressed and so ashamed. My roommate had been playing a Christian worship song, and hearing that music made me realize how distant I was from God.

I grew up knowing about Jesus; I understood I was a sinner who needed a savior at twelve years old, and I was even baptized at church. But I had wandered so far from God and was living my own independent way. That morning, I knew I needed to return to God. I opened my childhood Bible and read John 10:10 where Jesus says, "I have come that they may have life, and have it to the full." The life I was living wasn't full. It was empty.

That day, I got on my knees on that scratchy dorm carpet, and I asked Jesus to forgive me of my sin once again. I asked Him to take control of my whole life and make me into the woman I was supposed to be. When I got up off my knees with tears streaming down my face, I felt different inside. I knew the Holy Spirit was now leading and directing my life. I felt God's presence and love for me.

To this day, that passage in John means so much to me. Jesus is our Good Shepherd who will lead us and give us "life to the full." I also know that Jesus really was with me just as it says in John 1:12, "Yet to all who did receive him, to those who believed in his name, he gave the right to become children of God."

After this story, I might ask if the listener has ever felt like I had. I might also ask one of the best questions (see chapter 8) and whether the listener is on a spiritual journey, too, but has somehow been sidetracked like I was.

My second story of transformation involves growing in maturity in Christ, and I tell it because it includes a gospel presentation and an easy way to invite others into great conversation. I tell this story most of all. See if you can notice the before, during, and after scene, the inclusion of Scripture, and the invitation to the listener.

Story Two: Maturing

When I turned forty, I couldn't believe how bad I felt inside. I had what psychologist Lauren Slater calls, "the ache for something I cannot name." I was filled with jealousy and comparison about every other woman's perfect life. And I found myself fighting for a seat at all these tables I thought would bring me life: the thin and beautiful table, the rich and famous table, and the high achieving table.

But on a summer day in late July, I sat on a balcony as I read a passage of Scripture that would change nearly everything about me. In Ephesians 2, a man named Paul wrote a letter to encourage Christians with the essentials of everything they would need for their new life with Jesus. He wrote this: "As for you, you were dead in your transgressions and sins, in which you used to live when you followed the ways of this world and of the ruler of the kingdom of the air, the spirit who is now at work in those who are disobedient. All of us also lived among them at one time, gratifying the cravings of our flesh and following its desires and thoughts. Like the rest, we were by nature deserving of wrath. But because of his great love for us, God, who is rich in mercy, made us alive with Christ even when we were dead in transgressions—it is by grace you have been saved. And God raised us up with Christ and seated us with him in the heavenly realms in Christ Jesus . . . For it is by grace you have been saved, through faith—and this is not from yourselves, it is the gift of God— not by works, so that no one can boast. For we are God's handiwork, created in Christ Jesus to do good works, which God prepared in advance for us to do."

I noticed so many things about my life in that passage of Scripture. I was spiritually dead before knowing Jesus; I was following the path of the world and not God. I also knew that God saved me and made me alive in Christ. He rescued me because of Jesus and showed mercy and grace to me though I deserved His wrath.

But then I noticed that strange expression that God "raised me up with Christ and seated" me with Jesus. I noticed that "seated" is a past-tense verse—meaning it's already somehow true of me. This verse was telling me that I was already seated at the greatest table with the Greatest King. I didn't have to fight for a seat at the table anymore. I was already there.

And remember how I wanted to be thin, rich, and accomplished? My therapist called those the three A's: appearance, affluence, and achievement. Instead of fighting for the three A's, I now live a seated life. Seated people adore (and radiate the beauty of Christ instead of obsessing over their appearance); they access all the riches of God's kingdom (instead of worrying about affluence); and they abide (instead of achieving) to produce the good works God has prepared for them. I became a different person that July.

Have you ever struggled with fighting for a seat at the table? What do you think of this invitation from God to take our seat with Jesus?

What if you collected two or three life stories that showcase God's transforming work in your life? Not only can you use these naturally in conversation, but you can also pass these stories down to children and grandchildren who need to know these stories. Let's tell our stories as a way to "sing a new song" to the Lord. Psalm 96:2–3 offers this invitation: "Sing to the LORD, praise his name; proclaim his salvation day after day. Declare his glory among the nations, his marvelous deeds among all peoples." I cannot wait for your family, neighbors, and coworkers to hear the marvelous deeds the Lord has accomplished in your life.

YOUR SENT LIFE

Consider / Discuss

1. When was the last time a story—rather than just facts— changed your mind about something?

2. Why would it matter to include Scripture in your stories?

3. How does it make you feel when you read Mary Pipher's words that "you have something to say that no one else can say"?

4. What stories were you told that drew you closer to Jesus? Think about times you've listened to a personal testimony or heard about the Lord's work in someone else's life.

Steps of Faith:

1. If you could only tell two life stories to the next generation, which stories would you tell and why?

2. Begin writing a story of gospel transformation in just one page (that might take one to three minutes to share).

3. Locate the Scripture passages that best align with your story of transformation.

4. Write a few questions at the end of your story that could engage the listener and invite them to respond.

CHAPTER 10

Inviting a Response

If you declare with your mouth, "Jesus is Lord,"
and believe in your heart that God
raised him from the dead, you will be saved.

—Romans 10:9

I (Heather) recently shared with my sister something God has been teaching me most of all about living a sent life. It comes from a moment in Scripture that inspires how I now interact with those around me. In Matthew 16:13–16, Jesus begins a conversation with His disciples about who people say He is. The conversation moves from a general discussion to something personal, and it models the key piece in living a sent life. We read this:

> When Jesus came to the region of Caesarea Philippi, he asked his disciples, "Who do people say the Son of Man is?"
>
> They replied, "Some say John the Baptist; others say Elijah; and still others, Jeremiah or one of the prophets."
>
> "But what about you?" he asked. "Who do you say I am?"
>
> Simon Peter answered, "You are the Messiah, the Son of the living God."

When Jesus turns to Peter and says, "Who do you say I am?" my heart knows that question is the key question sent people ask those around them. *But what about you? Who do you say Jesus is?* But here's my problem: I can talk about spiritual things all day long. I can tell my stories of transformation. I can ask good questions. I can notice people. I can do all the things we've talked about in this book.

But I can struggle to turn to a person and ask the key question, "Now what does this mean to you? Who do you believe Jesus is?" In other words, while I can clearly explain how one can know God personally, I must, at some point, actually invite a person to respond.

I told my sister that I'm working on that question in my life. I'm working on taking all my training and all my convictions and turning to that person I've been praying for and engaging in spiritual conversations to ask them *what they now think*. I get so nervous. I do have to trust God each time I ask someone what they think about Jesus and the gospel.

So do I (Ashley). I suspect that many of us do. But Heather and I are increasingly convinced and convicted that as *sent ones*, we must do so. Inviting another to respond to Jesus lies at the core of our identity as *sent ones*. As sent ones, God invites us to preach the good news of the gospel so that others may respond to Jesus and ask Him to rescue them.

When do we do this? Do you ask the first time you speak with a person about spiritual things? Do you ask every time you speak with them about spiritual things? Do you need to wait until you have had many conversations over several months? That's a great question. As we've noted before, it depends on where a person is spiritually. If you shared the gospel with a friend who doesn't believe that God exists, knowing Him personally will probably seem really irrelevant to her. You'll likely need to help your friend believe God exists before a gospel conversation is fruitful. On the other hand, we all probably typically wait too long to share the gospel as we noted above.

To answer your question, here are three opportunities we take to share the gospel and invite someone to respond:

1. **When someone is ready to be invited to make a decision for Christ.** Based on the content of your conversations (whether many or just a few), you sense the person is interested in knowing God personally and knowing how to do so. When Heather saw her dental hygienist crying as she questioned how Heather knew God and prayed to Him, that was clearly a time to invite a response.

2. **When it comes up naturally in the course of a conversation.** The opportunity to share the gospel can naturally surface in a variety of ways. Perhaps the person is curious about faith and what others believe. Perhaps a person is really drawn to your life and wants to know why or how you live the way you do. Or perhaps someone shares about a difficulty in their life and you are able to share about the same or similar difficulty in your own life. You could do so, explain how God worked in your life, and then ask, "Have you ever experienced God in that way? Would you like to know how?"

3. **When you want someone to know and understand the content of the gospel.** This opportunity differs from the first two because the person may not be ready to make a decision. Instead, you simply want them to know and

understand the content of the gospel. Early on in my conversations with my neighbor Bill (the one with Scout, his dog), it became clear that Bill needed a clear explanation of the gospel to make sense of all that we were talking about. Additionally, walking through a clear presentation of the gospel helped Bill identify what he agreed with and what he disagreed with. It helped focus and direct our conversations tremendously.

Finally in all this, the leading of the Holy Spirit trumps everything. If He leads you to share the gospel and invite someone to respond (even if you think it is "too soon"), follow Him! Don't hold back. God may surprise you—and the person you are sharing with. Heather never imagined that her meeting with the woman who had questions about the spiritual words she used would lead to a moment when she asked, "What do you think about all this?" But it did.

When we ask someone if they want to hear more about having a relationship with Jesus, we use the tool *Would You Like to Know God Personally?* from Cru that you can read and download for free.[1] You can use any tool you like as long as you communicate clearly the essence of the gospel. When we are talking with someone and want to transition to sharing the gospel, we use the following question we learned as Cru staff: "Has anyone taken a few minutes to share with you a short outline of how you can know God personally? Would you like to take a few minutes now to do so?" The question communicates the attractiveness of the gospel and it honors the person by asking their permission first.

When a person agrees (most say "yes" in our experience), we open either *Would You Like to Know God Personally?* in the booklet form or use the mobile tool on Cru's GodTools app (available for free).[2] We then read through the content with the person we are sharing with. The last section of the tool asks questions that invite a person to respond to Jesus, so by reading through the whole tool together you will clearly explain the gospel *and* invite them to respond. This response takes the form of a prayer of invitation where a person expresses their desire to receive God's free gift of salvation by admitting their sins, asking for forgiveness, and inviting Jesus to come into their lives.

Finally, let's say you have shared the gospel with someone and they respond by receiving Jesus into their life. What next? First of all, celebrate! Celebrate with them. Celebrate with others. God just miraculously "delivered [your friend, family member, neighbor, coworker, someone] from the domain of darkness and transferred [him or her] to the kingdom of his beloved Son" (Col. 1:13–14 ESV). Next, help establish the new believer in his or her faith (Col. 2:7):

1. **Teach them the basics of walking with Jesus.**
2. **Invite them to church.**
3. **Introduce them to other believers.**
4. **Involve them in beginning their sent life.**
5. **Regularly meet with them to encourage their growth.**

As you invite those around you to respond to a gospel invitation, you'll participate in supernatural, eternal, divine activity. Your life will never be the same. You'll witness spiritual life beginning within a spiritually dead soul. You'll see the Holy Spirit summoning, convicting of sin, and enabling a response to Jesus. You'll sense the love of God like never before. And it will change you forever.

You'll remember your own story of God rescuing you. Your sent life will become a marvelous adventure of intimacy with Jesus.

YOUR SENT LIFE

Consider / Discuss

1. What resources do you need to invite a response to the gospel? Do you feel prepared?

2. What makes it so difficult to personally invite others to respond to Jesus?

3. Reflect on your experience so far in living a sent life. How did you respond emotionally to this chapter?

4. What do you need to believe about sharing your faith like this that would enable you to invite others to respond to the gospel?

Steps of Faith:

1. Begin thinking about who you might invite to respond to a gospel presentation.

2. Prepare your materials by downloading a gospel presentation like *Would You Like to Know God Personally?* either in the pdf form or through the GodTools app.

3. Talk to God about what keeps you from inviting others to receive Jesus into their lives. Is it fear of rejection? Is it that you don't feel prepared to answer questions? What keeps you from living a sent life?

4. Take your final step of faith to invite someone on your list to walk through a gospel presentation and respond.

PART 3

BEST PRACTICES FOR EVERYDAY EVANGELISM

CHAPTER 11

Great Expectations

The big question is whether you are going to be able to say a hearty yes to your adventure.

—Joseph Campbell

Very truly I tell you, whoever believes in me will do the works I have been doing, and they will do even greater things than these, because I am going to the Father.

—Jesus in John 14:12

Living a sent life represents a fundamental identity shift and new understanding of the call to a great mission. It's a way of experiencing Jesus and the world around us through a lens of *expectation*: we expect God to work around us; we expect that He still uses people to accomplish His kingdom building work; and we expect that God invites us—even you right now—into this magnificent work of introducing others to Jesus.

We see our homes, neighborhoods, work environments, and natural pathways differently; they now represent legitimate mission fields. And here, God sends us into the biblical missional roles as farmers, fishermen, ambassadors, and royal priests. We are hardworking, patient, confident, and authoritative as we proclaim the mystery of the gospel. We see others the same way Jesus does and care for them dearly. We ask great questions. We tell powerful stories of gospel transformation. We invite others to respond.

How will our hearts change in light of all we've learned? Do we now see the people in our lives as sovereignly placed there so we might proclaim the gospel to them? Do we now live with an eternal perspective wherever we go?

Can you imagine living in light of these expectations of God working? The best part of living a sent life is that we don't *have to try in our own power*. God is already working. He's already positioning, instructing, and empowering. We simply listen and cooperate.

If this sounds mystical or overly spiritual, it's not. It's nothing more than what we see in the book of Acts, for example. If you remember, the Holy Spirit *sends Ananias* to pray over Saul (9:17); He *sends men* to speak to Peter (10:19–21); He *sends Saul and Barnabas* on their way (13:4). Most notably, we see an incredible account of God's sending work in Acts 8:26–40. Notice the specificity of how *God sends Philip* to someone who needs to know about Jesus. We read this:

> Now an angel of the Lord said to Philip, "Go south to the road—the desert road—that goes down from Jerusalem to Gaza." So he started out, and on his way he met an Ethiopian eunuch, an important official in charge of all the treasury of the Kandake (which means "queen of the Ethiopians"). This man had gone to Jerusalem to worship, and on his way home was sitting in his chariot reading the Book of Isaiah the

prophet. The Spirit told Philip, "Go to that chariot and stay near it."

Then Philip ran up to the chariot and heard the man reading Isaiah the prophet. "Do you understand what you are reading?" Philip asked.

"How can I," he said, "unless someone explains it to me?" So he invited Philip to come up and sit with him."

Notice how the Holy Spirit directs Philip with clear instructions. I (Heather) am personally terrible with driving instructions, so I love how the Lord makes sure Philip knows which road to take (the desert road, the one going down from Jerusalem to Gaza). The Holy Spirit then tells Philip *exactly what to do*. The rest of the encounter tells us something about a successful evangelism strategy: Philip listens and asks a great question: *Do you understand what you are reading?*

The man shows Philip the passage from the book of Isaiah that has him stumped:

> "He was led like a sheep to the slaughter,
>   and as a lamb before its shearer is silent,
>   so he did not open his mouth.
> In his humiliation he was deprived of justice.
>   Who can speak of his descendants?
>   For his life was taken from the earth."

The eunuch asked Philip, "Tell me, please, who is the prophet talking about, himself or someone else?" Then Philip began with that very passage of Scripture and told him the good news about Jesus.

This passage in Acts encourages us to simply begin with the questions people have about what they're experiencing in life, what they've heard about God, or what confuses them about spiritual things. When Philip begins with the "very passage of Scripture" the man struggles with, notice how Philip begins to explain how the Scripture pointed to Jesus. It's the same technique Jesus Himself uses in Luke 4 after He enters the synagogue to begin teaching publicly. We read that "He stood up to read, and the scroll of the prophet Isaiah was handed to him" (Luke 4:16–17). Jesus reads this, and then notice His response:

> "The Spirit of the Lord is on me,
>> because he has anointed me
>> to proclaim good news to the poor.
> He has sent me to proclaim freedom for the prisoners
>> and recovery of sight for the blind,
> to set the oppressed free,
>> to proclaim the year of the Lord's favor."

Then he rolled up the scroll, gave it back to the attendant and sat down. The eyes of everyone in the synagogue were fastened on him. He began by saying to them, "Today this scripture is fulfilled in your hearing." (vv. 18–21)

You know you're following Jesus because He leads you to lost people.

I love how God supernaturally ordained that moment. He provided the person to hand Jesus the scroll of Isaiah, and it's that passage that allows Jesus to proclaim how He fulfills this prophecy.

God went ahead of both Philip and Jesus to ordain a special moment to advance the gospel. This same God goes ahead of us now to position us with people, in exact places, with problems we're uniquely equipped to explain in light of the gospel. We arrive with great questions, stories of gospel transformation, and Scripture that awakens the soul by the power of the Holy Spirit. And we always remember that God will do this. He is doing this.

I'll never forget the day I heard Darryl Smith, the former national director for Cru High School, explain to students one way they could know that they were following Jesus. Smith simply said, "You know you're following Jesus because He leads you to lost people."

You know you're following Jesus because He leads you to lost people.

WHAT MIGHT YOU EXPECT FROM LIVING THIS SENT LIFE?

Sent people expect God to lead them to people who need Jesus.
Sent people expect God to use them in the lives of others.
Sent people expect supernatural things to happen.

Henry Blackaby, in his Bible study workbook *Experiencing God: Knowing and Doing the Will of God*, writes this about his own experience with God. He writes that God "gives me plenty to do to fill each day with meaning and purpose. If I do everything He says, I will be in the center of His will when He wants to use me for a special assignment."[1] But does God want to use us? Yes! As Blackaby concludes: God "wants to involve you in His kingdom purposes. He wants to accomplish His work through you."[2]

As God begins to accomplish His work through you, you can also expect that your home and family will serve as "gospel outposts" in your community. When you think of an outpost, you might picture a military encampment, secluded from battle, where people gather for protection, planning, and refreshment. It's a safe and secure location. Your gospel presence in your community means people might come to you for aid and protection. Imagine setting up your home with the kind of provision and safe atmosphere to invite others in. Imagine your gospel outpost as working as an arm of your local church or missions group where you not only serve and gather those who don't know Jesus, but you also gather other like-minded believers to pray and prepare themselves for their sent lives.

When Ashley and I first married, our little apartment in Ann Arbor became a gospel outpost. Together we prayed for our lists of five people in our lives who did not yet know Jesus. We wanted to live sent lives, and we knew we weren't the only ones. We decided—along with a few dear friends—to begin a weekly night of prayer for those on our lists. Our gospel outpost served just a few of us—Ashley, Jeff, Amy, Rachel, Katrina, James, David, and me—at first. We'd sit in a circle in the living room and sip hot tea while each of us shared the names of those we wanted to know Jesus. Our cat, Bobbin, would curl up on Amy's lap. I'd refill teacups. We'd record names in our prayer journals. And then we'd pray earnestly for God to begin to move in their lives.

Word spread about our gospel outpost. Soon, more and more Christians began to come to our evangelism prayer meeting. I purchased more tea and washed more cups. We moved the couches.

People stood packed against the walls. We had groups praying for their friends in the bedroom, a closet, and even the bathroom. And then, God moved powerfully. Not only did some of the people on our lists pray to receive Christ, but

While nobody understands God's timing or how many He might bring to you who need to know Jesus, we do know that He desires to use you in the lives of others.

they also then came to join our gospel outpost to reach *their* friends.

One special evening, a fellow colleague asked about this strange gathering with hot tea and prayer. When I told her that we pray for people who don't yet know Jesus, she asked, "Can I come? I don't know Jesus. I would like to come for prayer." And she came. She sat right in our circle and we prayed for her. I'll never forget those special early years of our marriage based on this idea of simply praying for five people in your life who don't know Jesus.

You might start your own evening of prayer to invite a few Christian friends to share the burden of prayer for family members, work friends, or neighbors. At this simple gathering, you might read a passage of Scripture or sing to the Lord and then share your list of people. Then, you pray together either as a large group or in smaller groups if your group grows like ours did. You don't have to serve tea, but I liked having something to offer because of the passage in Acts 2:42–47 that describes a similar gospel outpost gathering. We read how the followers of Jesus gathered together:

> They devoted themselves to the apostles' teaching and to fellowship, to the breaking of bread and to prayer. Everyone was filled with awe at the many wonders and signs performed by the apostles. All the believers were together and had everything in common. They sold property and possessions to

give to anyone who had need. Every day they continued to meet together in the temple courts. They broke bread in their homes and ate together with glad and sincere hearts, praising God and enjoying the favor of all the people. And the Lord added to their number daily those who were being saved.

This passage always warms my heart. While Ashley and I didn't sell our property or give away all our possessions, it did feel like our home became their home as people made use of our bedroom and bathroom to pray! We didn't serve bread, but we did have tea (and sometimes chocolate chip cookies made by Rachel). We did indeed sit together with glad and sincere hearts. We did feel a deep friendship with all who gathered. And we did see how the Lord "added to [our] number . . . those who were being saved."

Sent people expect God to work like this. While nobody understands God's timing or how many He might bring to you who need to know Jesus, we do know that He desires to use you in the lives of others. We bring what we have, and He performs the miracles. Like the little boy who offered Jesus his five loaves and three fish in John 6:9, we supply whatever we can. For me, it was use of our small apartment and some tea, and God began to work.

As you bring God the resources He has given you to serve as a gospel presence and gospel outpost, you'll begin to bless those around you. Recently, Ashley and I remembered a deeply convicting and deeply challenging question that invited us to reorient our lives back to our sent identity:

What would change in your community or workplace if you were no longer there?

This question allowed us to think about what we offer to those around us. It made us wonder what vital aid or blessing would end

If we left. We thought of a family down the street who moved away after several years. This was the family who hosted an open house of hot cider and pizza on Halloween. This was the family who hosted a huge catered brunch and Easter egg hunt for the neighbors. This was the family who was the first to deliver a present to us when our cat died and the family who gathered everyone together to make sure nobody was lonely or left out. They were generous, fun-loving, and always available. They hosted more meals for families on our street than I can remember. When they left, it felt like the street went dark for a few months. We missed them on Halloween and on Easter, especially. They've been gone for years, and we all still talk about them and how they blessed us with their generosity.

Can you imagine if God truly used you to change a community? Perhaps we've been thinking too small. What if your *whole city* changed and came to the Lord because of your willingness to live a sent life? And why not dream big? After all, Paul writes in Ephesians 3:20 (NLT): "Now all glory to God, who is able, through his mighty power at work within us, to accomplish infinitely more than we might ask or think." We serve a God who can do infinitely more than we even know how to ask or think.

YOUR SENT LIFE

Consider / Discuss

1. Have you had a moment like Philip in Acts where you felt God leading you to a person who needed to hear about Jesus? What happened?

2. Have you ever experienced the kind of fellowship described in Acts 2?

3. What would change in your community if you were no longer there? What would you *want* to change if you were no longer there? Rather than feeling despair if you feel insignificant in your neighborhood or workplace, ask the Lord how He might use you to bless the people in those spaces.

4. Could you imagine your home as a "gospel outpost"? What comes to mind when you think of that phrase?

Steps of Faith:

1. Record supernatural moments of your sent life.

2. Begin mapping out how your home might become a "gospel outpost."

3. Gather with three or four other Christians to begin praying for those who don't yet know Jesus.

4. Write down your "big dream" of living a sent life. Will you pray for revival for a specific person or group? Will you commit to pray for your whole city, state, and region?

CHAPTER 12

Great Surrender

Do you know why you are where you are? Who you are?
God has made you that way to save many lives.
It is your destiny. In this incredible moment,
God has positioned you to save many lives.

—Ron Hutchcraft in "Rescue the Dying"

Living a sent life requires surrender.

You won't live anymore like the rest of the world.

Your life won't make sense to other people.

And you may struggle with this surrendered kind of living.

I (Heather) remember clearly the day my heart shifted toward a deeper call to surrender to living a sent life. Our dear friend came to visit us on a snowy evening over twenty years ago. He wanted us to hear a message called "Rescue the Dying" he had heard from a man named Ron Hutchcraft. Our friend insisted. So we decided to drive around in our car to listen to this message on a cassette tape (that's how long ago this was!).

Hutchcraft begins by telling a story of going hiking to see this beautiful waterfall, but you could only see it if you left the safe, dry ground and traveled along a dangerous pipeline. He says, "I knew where I stood. I had gone as far as I could go safely." He pauses and says, "So has Christianity." Hutchcraft began to talk about the risks now involved and the danger of only staying safe and not moving into the kind of surrender required to live lives on mission to rescue lost people. He says,

> The problem is that if we just continue to go, we will continue to lose our neighbors and friends to the powers of darkness. Because while we have built the largest Christian subculture in the history of the church . . . we can go to our meetings and our beautiful buildings, but while we have built the largest Christian subculture in history and say we're winning, we lost our culture. This is post-Christian America. . . . If we just keep doing what we've been doing, we will leave most of our generation unreached for Jesus Christ. And I believe that there are many people . . . who have in their hearts a deep restlessness. I have sensed it.[1]

I began to shiver from the cold but also because of the gravity of the call to evangelism. Then, Hutchcraft said the words I'll never forget: "You didn't pick when you lived. God picked you for now."[2] And although he delivered this message in 1999—when he believed this was "the most reachable moment in American history" because of advances in technology, I can only imagine what he might say today. As Ashley and I continued to listen to the final words of "Rescue the Dying," we heard these questions: "Do you know why you are where you are? Who you are? God has made you that way to save many lives. It is your destiny. In this incredible moment, God has positioned you to save many lives."[3]

In this incredible moment, God has positioned you to save many lives.

Tears formed in my eyes. Although I now had a PhD and could do so many important things with that degree, I thought of nothing more important than living a sent life. No matter what it cost me, I would let Jesus send me. Ron Hutchcraft concludes by articulating everything I feared. He says, "I've never known anyone who was rescued by a rescuer who chose comfort. You cannot rescue dying people from a safe place. If you follow Jesus, you'll find yourself in a sea of lost people, and you will lay down your life for them. Jesus says to us, 'I am coming to rescue them, and I am sending you.'"

Ashley and I knew it was true. We could affirm, as Hutchcraft did, that "the central passion of the Lord is to rescue." We wanted, now more than ever before, to join that rescue mission.

And now, we invite you once again, to live a *sent life* for the rest of your life.

YOUR SENT LIFE

Consider / Discuss

1. How does it make you feel to know that God picked you for now? For right where you live?

2. Do you believe that we are losing neighbors and friends to the powers of darkness? How does that darkness look in your particular community?

3. Do you agree that the central passion of the Lord is to rescue? How do you know?

4. What do you think you'll have to give up in order to live the sent life God asks us to?

Steps of Faith:

1. What would it look like for you to leave a life of comfort to rescue lost people?

2. How is the Lord asking you to more deeply surrender to Him to live a sent life?

3. Write a prayer of surrender and expectation about your new sent life. What do you want to confess to God, tell God, and ask God?

4. What does your new sent life look like? What is your next faith step?

Acknowledgments

While the Lord sent so many people into our lives to shape our sent identity, we'd like to first thank our parents—Curtis and Kitty Holleman and Brad and Linda Brown. We also want to thank the churches that first shaped us including Plymouth Haven Baptist Church in Alexandria, Virginia; Wake Chapel Christian Church in Fuquay-Varina, North Carolina; and Grace Bible Church and Knox Presbyterian Church in Ann Arbor, Michigan. Special thanks to those whom God originally sent to pour into our lives to help us know Jesus better and follow Him into the lives of others: my sister Melissa Kish, Cecil and Lynn Sanders, the McKnights, Jim Lindsay, Mark Poindexter, Bob Johnson, David Brown, Dave and Jenny McCreary, Rev. Ron and Louise Marion, Roderick Black, Lynda Smethurst, Sandi Lavery Taylor, Elizabeth Perhson, Libby and Jim Miller, Jimboy Miller, Laura Hollowell, Matt Hardy, Chuck and Dianne Roeper, Michele Ashton, Carey Wallace, Robb Wilson, Bob and Ronda Adgate, and our "gospel outpost" friends including Rachel Hadley, Amy Litwak, Jeff Brake, Katrina Walsemann, David Plate, and James MacKay. Thank you to Jennifer Rich, Dr. Gregory Hocott, Patrice Pederson, and our Grace Bible Kaleo Group. We also thank Rick and Sonya Hove,

Marc and Patty Rutter, Jay and Laurie Lorenzen, Bill and Jan Hager, John and Cindy Peterson, Rich and Bonnie McGee, and Randy and Pam Newman. Thank you to Vic and Kay King, John and Sandy Mackin, Aaron and Amy Henning, Erik and JoAnn Foley-DeFiore and Brooke and Brian Barnett. Finally, we wish to honor our beautiful daughters, Sarah and Kate, who embraced our lives as a sent family.

Notes

Chapter 1: Believing That God Is at Work Around You

1. See Bill Bright, "Have You Heard of the Four Spiritual Laws?," https://crustore .org/media/Four_Spiritual_Laws_English_.pdf.
2. Barna Report Produced in Partnership with Alpha USA: *Reviving Evangelism: Current Realities That Demand a New Vision for Sharing Faith* (Ventura, CA: Barna Group, 2019), 10.

Chapter 2: Believing the Gospel

1. Sally Lloyd Jones, *The Jesus Storybook Bible: Every Story Whispers His Name* (Grand Rapids: ZonderKidz, 2007).

Chapter 3: Believing God's Titles and Job Descriptions for Your Life

Epigraph: Robert Coleman, *The Master Plan of Evangelism* (Grand Rapids: Revell, 2010), 89.

1. Rick Hove and Heather Holleman, *A Grander Story: An Invitation to Christian Professors* (Orlando: CruPress, 2017).
2. Barna Report Produced in Partnership with Alpha USA, *Reviving Evangelism: Current Realities that Demand a New Vision for Sharing Faith* (Ventura, CA: Barna Group, 2019), 10.
3. Matthew George Easton, "Ambassador," *Easton's Bible Dictionary*, https:// www.biblestudytools.com/dictionaries/eastons-bible-dictionary/ambassador .html.
4. Charles Spurgeon, "God Beseeching Sinners by His Ministers," Sermon No. 1,124, *Metropolitan Tabernacle Pulpit*, vol. 19, July 27, 1873, https://www .spurgeongems.org/vols19-21/chs1124.pdf.
5. Francis Frangipane, *Spiritual Discernment and the Mind of Christ* (Cedar Rapids, IA: Arrow Publications, 2013) as quoted by Ministries of Francis Frangipane, Facebook post, https://www.facebook.com/francisfrangipane/, Sept. 11, 2019.
6. Meg Bucher, "What This Irish Blessing Means: 'May the Road Rise Up to Meet You,'" September 19, 2018, https://www.crosswalk.com/faith/prayer/what-this-irish-blessing-means-may-the-road-rise-up-to-meet-you.html.

7. Charles Spurgeon, *The Treasury of David* (Peabody, MA: Hendrickson Publishers, 1990), 431.

8. Charles Spurgeon, "Come from the Four Winds, O Breath!," *Metropolitan Tabernacle Pulpit*, vol. 38, Sermon No. 2246, May 15, 1890, https://www.ccel.org/ccel/spurgeon/sermons38.x.html.

9. Charles Spurgeon, "The Mustard Seed: A Sermon for the Sabbath-School Teacher," *Metropolitan Tabernacle Pulpit*, vol. 35, Sermon No. 2110, October 20, 1889, https://www.spurgeon.org/resource-library/sermons/the-mustard-seed-a-sermon-for-the-sabbath-school-teacher#flipbook/.

10. Stephen Lawson, "The Convicting Power of Scripture," *The One Passion Blog*, May 18, 2015, http://www.onepassionministries.org/blog/2015/5/17/the-convicting-power-of-scripture.

11. *Reviving Evangelism*, 11.

Chapter 4: Believing in Supernatural Power

1. Bill Bright, "Success in Evangelism," Cru, Evangelism," adapted from Bill Bright, *How You Can Be a Fruitful Witness*, Transferable Concepts, https://www.cru.org/us/en/train-and-grow/transferable-concepts/be-a-fruitful-witness.6.html.

2. Keith Davy, "Satisfied?," Cru, https://www.cru.org/us/en/train-and-grow/spiritual-growth/satisfied.html.

Chapter 5: The World We're Sent Into

1. "In U.S., Decline of Christianity Continues at a Rapid Pace," *Pew Research Center*, October 17, 2019, https://www.pewforum.org/2019/10/17/in-u-s-decline-of-christianity-continues-at-rapid-pace/.

2. Harriet Sherwood, "Religion: Why Faith Is Becoming More and More Popular," *The Guardian*, August 27, 2018, https://www.theguardian.com/news/2018/aug/27/religion-why-is-faith-growing-and-what-happens-next.

3. "Global Christianity—A Report on the Size and Distribution of the World's Christian Population," *Pew Research Center*, December 19, 2011, https://www.pewforum.org/2011/12/19/global-christianity-exec/.

4. Randy Newman, *Unlikely Converts* (Grand Rapids: Kregel, 2019), 33.

5. Doug Pollock, *God Space: Where Spiritual Conversations Happen Naturally* (Loveland, CO: Group, 2009), 44.

Chapter 7: Gathering and Caring

Epigraph: Ellie Polack, "New Cigna Study Reveals Loneliness at Epidemic Levels in America," Cigna, May 1, 2018, https://www.cigna.com/newsroom/news-releases/2018/new-cigna-study-reveals-loneliness-at-epidemic-levels-in-america.

1. Heather Holleman, *Seated with Christ: Living Freely in a Culture of Comparison* (Chicago: Moody, 2015).

2. Hannah Schulze, "Loneliness: An Epidemic?," Science in the News, Harvard University, April 16, 2018, http://sitn.hms.harvard.edu/flash/2018/loneliness-an-epidemic/.

3. Polack, "New Cigna Study Reveals Loneliness at Epidemic Levels in America."

4. Casper ter Kuile and Angie Thurston, "How We Gather," 2015, https://caspertk.files.wordpress.com/2015/04/how-we-gather1.pdf, 6.

5. Barna Report Produced in Partnership with Alpha USA, *Reviving Evangelism: Current Realities that Demand a New Vision for Sharing Faith* (Ventura, CA: Barna Group, 2019), 24.

Chapter 8: The Easiest Questions to Ask

1. Todd B. Kashdan et al., "The Five-Dimensional Curiosity Scale: Capturing the Bandwidth of Curiosity and Identifying Four Unique Subgroups of Curious People," *Journal of Research in Personality* 73 (2018): 130–49.

2. Todd B. Kashdan and Michael F. Steger, "Curiosity and Pathways to Well-Being and Meaning in Life: Traits, States, and Everyday Behaviors," *Motivation and Emotion* 31, no. 3 (November 2007): 159–73.

3. "Dr. Todd Kashdan on Building Curiosity," YouTube, February 16, 2012, https://www.youtube.com/watch?v=Bv3wQ94G6xE.

4. Kashdan and Steger, ibid.

5. Todd Kashdan, quoted in Jill Suttie, "Why Curious People Have Better Relationships," *Greater Good*, May 31, 2017, https://greatergood.berkeley.edu/article/item/why_curious_people_have_better_relationships.

6. Kashdan et al., "The Five-Dimensional Curiosity Scale."

7. Suttie, "Why Curious People Have Better Relationships."

8. "Only One-Third of Young Adults Feel Cared For by Others," Barna Group, October 15, 2019, https://www.barna.com/research/global-connection-isolation/.

9. Roger Schwarz, "Being Genuinely Curious," Roger Schwarz and Associates, May 2005, http://www.schwarzassociates.com/managing-performance/being-genuinely-curious/.

10. "Faculty Faith Stories," Faculty Commons Interview, 2015.

11. Ibid.

Chapter 9: The Easiest Story to Tell

Epigraph: Peter Guber, "The Inside Story," *Psychology Today*, March 15, 2011, https://www.psychologytoday.com/sg/articles/201103/the-inside-story?collection=132608.

1. David Aaker and Jennifer L. Aaker, "What Are Your Signature Stories?," *California Management Review* 58 (2016): 2.

2. Guber, "The Inside Story."

3. Mary Pipher, *Writing to Change the World: An Inspiring Guide for Transforming the World with Words* (New York: Penguin, 2006), 45.

4. Paul J. Zak, "Why Inspiring Stories Make Us React: The Neuroscience of Narrative," *Cerebrum: The Dana Forum on Brain Science* 2 (2015): www.ncbi.nlm.nih.gov/pmc/articles/PMC4445577/.

5. Nancy Duarte, "How to Tell a Story," March 21, 2013, https://www.youtube.com/watch?v=9JrRQ1oQWQk.

6. Guber, "The Inside Story."

7. Ibid.

8. Ibid.

9. Erik Raymond, "The Word of God Is Powerful, It Is Undefeatable," The Gospel Coalition, February 24, 2014, https://www.thegospelcoalition.org/blogs/erik-raymond/the-word-of-god-is-powerful-it-is-undefeatable/.

Chapter 10: Inviting a Response

1. "Would You Like to Know God Personally?" is available as a PDF at https://crustore.org/downloads/would.pdf.

2. GodTools app available for free download or see GodToolsApp.com for product information and instructions.

Chapter 11: Great Expectations

1. Henry Blackaby and Claude King, *Experiencing God: Knowing and Doing the Will of God* (Nashville: Lifeway Press, 1990), 11.

2. Ibid., 18.

Chapter 12: Great Surrender

Epigraph: Ron Hutchcraft, "Rescue the Dying," https://www.cru.org/us/en/train-and-grow/share-the-gospel/evangelism-principles/rescue-the-dying.html.

1. Ron Hutchcraft, "Rescue the Dying."

2. Ibid.

3. Ibid.

Resource List

While many excellent resources exist on talking to others about Jesus, we've picked the books and tools that have most shaped our own journey into living a sent life. For further training, tools, and ways to help new believers grow in their faith, visit the *Train and Grow* resource at Cru.org.

Bill Bright, *Would You Like to Know God Personally?* Visit https://crustore.org/downloads/would.pdf.

Bill Bright, *The Spirit-Filled Life*, https://www.cru.org/us/en/train-and-grow/spiritual-growth/the-spirit-filled-life.html.

Robert E. Coleman, *The Master Plan of Evangelism* (Revell, 2010).

Tim Keller, *The Reason for God: Belief in an Age of Skepticism* (Penguin, 2009).

Randy Newman, *Bringing the Gospel Home: Witnessing to Family Members, Close Friends, and Others Who Know You Well* (Crossway, 2011) and *Questioning Evangelism: Engaging People's Hearts the Way Jesus Did* (Kregel, 2017).

Doug Pollock, *God Space: Where Spiritual Conversations Happen Naturally* (Group, 2009).

More from Heather Holleman

978-0-8024-1687-2

978-0-8024-1487-8

978-0-8024-1343-7

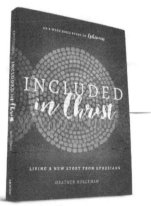

Included in Christ is an in-depth, 8-week study of Ephesians designed to facilitate honest sharing and help women internalize their identity in Christ. It guides women in telling their "shadow stories" and rewriting those according to the provisions they have in Christ. It offers a wonderful balance of community, connectedness, and spiritual nourishment.

978-0-8024-1591-2